THE INDIE AUTHOR'S GUIDE TO FAST DRAFTING YOUR NOVEL

THE INDIE AUTHOR'S GUIDE

MONIQUE JOINER SIEDLAK

THE INDIE AUTHOR'S GUIDE TO FAST DRAFTING

How to Write Your Novel in Just a Few Weeks

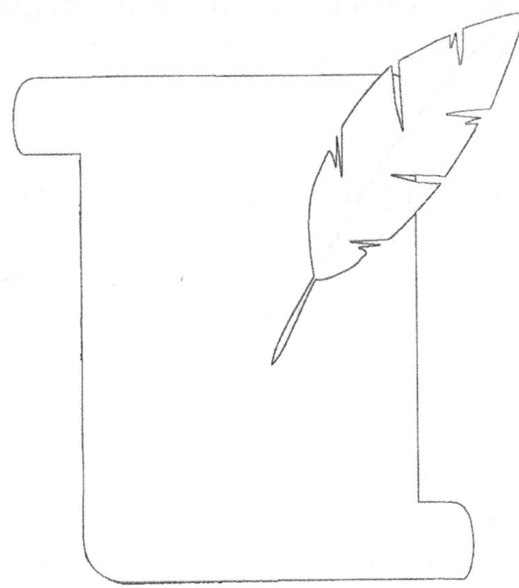

MONIQUE JOINER SIEDLAK

ISBN 978-1-956319-99-6 (Paperback)

ISBN 978-1-961362-00-0 (Hardback)

ISBN 978-1-956319-98-9 (eBook)

Cover Design by LSK Designs

lskbookcoverdesign.com

Published by Oshun Publications

9 Old Kings Road STE. 123 #1038; Palm Coast, FL 32137

www.oshunpublications.com

CONTENTS

INTRODUCTION TO FAST DRAFTING

An Overview of the Fast Drafting Process

Completing the first draft of any literary work is a decisive landmark in a writer's journey. Every sentence and paragraph are stepping stones, leading closer to the grand finale—a complete manuscript. With each page turned, the writer is enveloped in a whirlwind of emotions: joy, self-doubt, triumph, and trepidation. Nevertheless, amidst the chaos, a sense of accomplishment lingers—the knowledge that they have birthed something extraordinary, a creation that is uniquely theirs. This stage often poses challenges and obstacles, hindering progress and dampening motivation. This chapter aims to guide and empower writers through fast drafting by setting realistic goals and surmounting common hurdles.

Fast drafting is an approach to writing that focuses on completing a draft quickly and efficiently. Fast drafting has numerous benefits; writers should employ practical tips to implement this technique. Fast drafting involves setting aside a specific period to write a novel's first draft. The goal is to prioritize speed and momentum over perfectionism during the drafting stage. By doing so, writers can tap into their creativity, overcome self-doubt, and prevent the project from languishing in the planning stage. It's important to set tangible objectives for fast drafting. This involves determining a target word count or chapter count for the draft and breaking it down into manageable milestones. With specific goals in mind, writers can track their progress and maintain motivation throughout the process.

To facilitate fast drafting, you should create a structured writing routine. This includes setting aside dedicated writing time and establishing a consistent schedule (Kieffer, 2021). By making writing a regular habit, writers can build momentum and minimize distractions. Another crucial aspect of fast drafting is the utilization of effective outlining techniques. Develop a loose outline that provides a roadmap for the story while allowing room for discovery and improvisation. By having a general direction for the plot and characters, writers can stay on track and avoid getting stuck in a rut. It would help to suppress the inner critic during the quick drafting period. Writers are encouraged to prioritize writing the story on paper rather than worrying about perfect prose or editing.

This allows for a more unrestricted flow of ideas and prevents self-doubt from hindering progress. It is worth acknowledging that every writer is distinct, and what works for one may not work for another. A writer should be encouraged to experiment with various techniques and find the approach that best suits their writing style and preferences. Fast drafting is an approach to writing that prioritizes speed, momentum, and progress. By setting realistic goals, establishing a writing routine, utilizing effective outlining techniques, and silencing the inner critic, writers can complete a first draft quickly and efficiently. Ultimately, fast drafting allows writers to tap into their wellspring of creative juices, conquer self-doubt, and bring their narratives to life.

Advantages of Fast Drafting

By embracing the fast drafting approach, writers can preserve their enthusiasm and momentum, avoiding the ominous snares of overthinking and self-doubt that often become burdensome in the early stages of writing. Fast drafting enables writers to unbridle their creativity and achieve a sense of accomplishment as they progress toward their writing aims. The upside of fast drafting your novel is diverse and can significantly benefit your writing process. This section will explore the advantages of embracing the fast drafting approach.

Completing a full first draft quickly is one of the primary advantages of fast drafting. Unlike traditional drafting methods, where it may take months or even years to finish a manuscript, fast drafting enables writers to expedite the process and complete their first draft in a relatively short period—a few months or weeks. The ability to finish a draft rapidly offers numerous benefits to authors. Firstly, it provides a tremendous sense of accomplishment. Seeing an entire story unfold, writers experience a surge of satisfaction and realization, knowing that they have successfully brought their inner world to life in the outside world. This achievement fuels enthusiasm and boosts confidence, spurring them to continue their creative journey with increased enthusiasm.

Moreover, fast drafting allows writers to push through the various stages of doubt, self-criticism, and perfectionism that often plague the early drafting process. By prioritizing speed and forward momentum, writers are encouraged to silence their inner nay-sayer and focus on getting the story down in black and white. This freedom from obsessive self-editing and pursuit of perfection helps novelists break free from the cycle of endless revisions and move forward with their creative inspiration.

Additionally, completing a full first draft faster provides a tangible milestone in their writing journey. It offers them a solid foundation to build and refine their work in subsequent revisions. By having a complete draft, authors comprehensively understand their story's structure, characters, and plotlines, enabling them to make more informed decisions during editing. This initial draft becomes a framework for further development and refinement, facilitating the creation of a polished final product. One's ability to quickly complete a full first draft through fast drafting brings writers a profound sense of triumph, motivation, and progress. By focusing on the story and bypassing the pursuit of perfection, writers can overcome doubts and self-criticism, ultimately reaching a significant milestone in their writing journey. This journey of refining and perfecting is not without its challenges. Doubts may creep in, whispering in the writer's ear, questioning their choices, and dampening their morale. However, amidst the upheaval of uncertainty, the writer stands tall, fueled by a passion that burns brighter than any doubt. They forge ahead, armed with determination and a fierce commitment to their craft.

When you fast draft, you prioritize the story's forward momentum over perfecting every scene or paragraph (Robson, n.d.). This means you don't spend excessive time editing and polishing sections that may ultimately be changed or cut during the revision process. You maximize your writing time by saving extensive editing until the end. Fast drafting saves valuable time by prioritizing the story's forward momentum rather than getting caught up in excessive editing during the initial drafting stage. This approach ensures that you do not spend unnecessary effort polishing scenes or paragraphs that may undergo significant changes or even be axed altogether during the revision process.

By keeping detailed editing in your back pocket for later stages, fast drafting maximizes the efficiency of writing time. Instead of continuously refining and perfecting every sentence, you focus on capturing your ideas, characters, and plotlines without self-editing constraints. This mindset allows for a more fluid and uninhibited creative process, as you can explore different avenues and experiment with various narrative elements. As a result, you can progress swiftly through your drafts, dedicating your time and energy to advancing the story rather than getting stuck in the cycle of fine-tuning individual sections. This saves time and maintains the momentum and flow of the writing process, preventing the writer from becoming mired in self-doubt or losing sight of the narrative's bigger picture.

Furthermore, by throwing extensive editing on the back burner until later stages, writers gain a fresh perspective when they revisit their drafts for revision. This separation allows them to approach the work more objectively, making it easier to identify areas that need improvement, restructuring, or elimination. It also prevents the writer from becoming too attached to specific scenes or paragraphs that may not serve the story's overall purpose or theme. In essence, fast drafting streamlines the writing process by minimizing time spent on unnecessary editing during the initial drafting stage. By prioritizing the story's forward momentum, writers can use their writing time efficiently, maintain the flow of creativity, and gain a fresh perspective for subsequent revisions. This approach ultimately leads to a more dynamic and engaging final draft.

Fast drafting is a powerful method for writers to overcome fears that impede their progress. It demands perseverance and determination, encouraging writers to push past their insecurities and embrace the belief that they can produce a complete manuscript. By actively engaging in the writing process and focusing on completing the draft, writers build resilience and develop a strong work ethic. They learn to confront their doubts head-on, refusing to let them hinder their creative output. Fast drafting enables writers to hush their inner critic, which often whispers self-doubt and self-criticism. It spurs them to let go of the need for perfection and instead prioritizes getting the story down on paper. This practice of pushing forward despite doubts and fears strengthens writers' faith in their writing prowess. It builds confidence in their ability to produce a complete manuscript.

As the ink spills and the words flow like a gushing river, artists are immersed in a whirlwind of emotions and ideas. Amid this creative frenzy, they discover a hidden reservoir of resilience and determination that propels them forward. They witness firsthand their capacity to overcome obstacles and persist in facing challenges. This experience fosters a sense of empowerment and a belief in their ability to see a writing project through to completion. Furthermore, fast drafting allows writers to develop a habit of consistent action. By kicking to the curb doubts and fears, they establish a routine of showing up and coming up with words on the page, regardless of any internal resistance. This commitment to regular writing practice builds momentum and reinforces authors' confidence in their ability to produce work consistently.

Fast drafting is a transformative practice that enables writers to confront and seize qualms. By adopting this attitude, authors build resilience, a strong work ethic, and confidence in their writing ability. Through consistent action and the belief in their creative potential, novelists can unlock their full writing potential and breathe life into their stories. Maintaining writing momentum is critical to fast drafting, contributing to completing a long-form project like a novel. Fast drafting techniques emphasize the importance of consistent forward motion, allowing writers to avoid getting stuck or losing enthusiasm during the writing process. One of the critical advantages of fast drafting is its ability to prevent stagnation. By not dwelling excessively on individual scenes or chapters, writers avoid becoming mired in endless revisions or fixating on perfecting every aspect of their work. Instead, they maintain a steady pace, continuously moving forward with the story. This momentum ensures that writers remain engaged and motivated throughout the writing process.

Fast drafting encourages writers to resist the temptation to rework and polish previous sections constantly. Instead, they focus on advancing the narrative, developing characters, and exploring plotlines. This emphasis on progress keeps the artistic energy flowing and prevents the project from stalling. Writers who maintain momentum are less likely to suffer the dreaded writer's block or feel overwhelmed by the project's magnitude. The constant progress achieved through fast drafting fuels incentive and drive. As writers witness their stories taking shape and the word count steadily increasing, they experience a sense of accomplishment and excitement. This motivation becomes a driving force, spurring them to continue writing and driving them closer to the finish line.

Additionally, maintaining writing momentum enhances the general quality of the work. When authors maintain a consistent flow, ideas flow more freely, and creativity flourishes. By avoiding long breaks or extended periods of inactivity, novelists can sustain their connection with the story and the characters, resulting in a more cohesive and immersive reading experience for their audience.

Additionally, the continuous progress achieved through fast drafting allows novelists to identify and address potential issues or inconsistencies in a timely manner. A complete draft gives them a holistic view of the novel, enabling them to make more informed decisions during the revision process. This helps them refine and polish their masterpiece with a deeper narrative comprehension. Fast drafting enables writers to maintain writing momentum by consistently moving forward without getting stuck or losing enthusiasm. By avoiding excessive revisions and focusing on progress, writers remain engaged with the story, fuel their impetus, and enhance the quality of their work.

The continuous forward motion facilitates the identification and resolution of issues, leading to a more refined and polished final product. Fast drafting offers several advantages that can positively impact your writing process. You can make significant strides in your writing journey by quickly completing a full first draft, saving time on unnecessary editing, breaking the editing-as-you-go loop, overcoming doubts and fears, and maintaining writing momentum. Embracing the fast drafting approach allows you to tap into your creativity, build discipline, and skyrocket your project forward with vigor and enthusiasm.

How to Set Realistic Goals for Fast Drafting

Setting realistic goals is like charting a course through treacherous waters. Just as a skilled captain navigates their ship, the writer steers their words with precision and care. Without clear objectives, writers can quickly become overwhelmed or lose focus. This chapter will delve into strategies for setting realistic goals, whether they are related to word count, time-based targets, or specific project milestones. By establishing attainable goals, writers can stay motivated and track their progress effectively. It is wise to set clear and measurable goals. Vague or overly broad goals can be overwhelming and hinder progress. Instead, writers should define their objectives precisely and quantifiable, allowing for clear benchmarks to track their progress. Fast drafting is an invaluable technique for rapidly progressing your writing project. It involves writing the first draft of your novel, short story, or novella as swiftly as possible, allowing characters, arcs, and plotlines to take shape while focusing on the big-picture ideas rather than getting caught up in fine details.

It's important to consider the following tips to set realistic goals for fast drafting. Create a scene map instead of a traditional outline or chronological chapter list. This approach benefits writers of non-linear stories who may only know the exact order of scenes later. Begin by jotting down key scenes and significant character moments you know will appear in your book. This map will serve as a flexible guide as you fast-draft your story. Recognize that each writer responds differently to goal-setting. Spend some time observing and comprehending your writing routines and tendencies. Consider the type of writer you are, how you emotionally react when faced with concrete goals, and when you can realistically allocate time for writing in your schedule. By aligning your goals with your tendencies and availability, you can set writing goals that are both effective and achievable.

By incorporating these tips into your fast drafting process, you can establish realistic goals that suit your writing style and schedule (Ren, 2019). Remember, the key is to prioritize progress and allow your ideas to flow while minimizing distractions and focusing on the bigger picture. With a well-defined scene map and an understanding of your writing patterns, you'll be well-equipped to embark on a successful fast-drafting odyssey.

Common Fast Drafting Problems

Fast drafting is like traversing a rugged mountain trail. Every step forward is met with rocky terrain and steep ascents, testing the writer's endurance and resolve. The path may be treacherous, filled with unforeseen obstacles and tangled thickets of self-doubt. Nevertheless, like an intrepid hiker, the writer presses on, fueled by their determination and unwavering passion. Common obstacles can arise, such as a lack of structure, flat characters, inconsistent voice, pacing problems, or weak endings. This section will provide insights and practical solutions to overcome these obstacles. By addressing these issues, head-on, writers can refine their fast drafts and create a solid foundation for future revisions. Next, we will address common issues writers encounter during the fast drafting process. We will provide insights and actionable ideas to help you overcome these obstacles and enhance the quality of your first draft.

One familiar problem writers face is needing more structure in their first draft. This can result in a meandering plot or a disjointed narrative. It would help if you began by outlining the main story beats and organizing the plot coherently before starting the fast draft. A clear roadmap can help writers maintain focus and ensure a more cohesive storyline.

Another area for improvement is the presence of flat or underdeveloped characters. Writers should invest time in character development by creating detailed character profiles and understanding their motivations, desires, and conflicts. Writers can create more engaging and relatable protagonists and supporting casts by giving characters depth and complexity.

Maintaining a consistent narrative voice is essential in a first draft. Writers often face challenges maintaining the same tone and style throughout the story. A great idea is reading the work aloud to identify inconsistencies and make necessary adjustments to ensure a consistent voice that aligns with the story's genre, tone, and intended audience.

Pacing issues can arise when the story feels too slow or rushed. To address this, assess the pacing at crucial moments in the plot and adjust the narrative accordingly. Writers can consider adding or removing scenes, adjusting the length of dialogue exchanges, or inserting moments of tension and conflict to create a more balanced and engaging pace.

Weak or unsatisfying endings are common in first drafts. Writers often struggle with delivering a compelling and emotionally resonant conclusion. Revisit the story's themes and ensure the end aligns with the narrative arc, creating a sense of closure while leaving room for future possibilities or unanswered questions to maintain reader interest.

Nonetheless, I intend to highlight these common first-draft problems and provide practical solutions. By focusing on structure, character development, consistent voice, pacing, and satisfying endings, novelists can overcome these challenges and enhance the quality of their fast draft. Taking the time to revise and polish the first draft is like a master sculptor meticulously chiseling away at a rough block of marble. With each chisel stroke, the sculptor unveils the hidden beauty within, refining the raw material into a masterpiece. Similarly, the writer approaches their initial draft discerningly, carving away unnecessary words, reshaping sentences, and refining the narrative flow.

Key Takeaways

Completing a literary work's first draft is a momentous milestone, filled with a rollercoaster of emotions. It's an odyssey that brings both joy and self-doubt. Still, ultimately, it is a testament to the writer's ability to create something unique. Fast drafting is a practical approach to navigating challenges and moving the project forward.

By emphasizing efficiency and speed, it taps into creativity, overcomes self-doubt, and prevents the work from stalling. Setting tangible objectives and tracking progress are crucial elements of fast drafting. Establishing a structured writing routine is also essential. By dedicating specific time to writing and maintaining a consistent schedule, writers build momentum and minimize distractions.

Additionally, effective outlining techniques provide a skeleton for the story while allowing room for improvisation. Finally, during the fast drafting process, it's essential to prioritize writing the story rather than perfecting the prose. This approach focuses on progress and allows for revisions and refinement in later stages. With these things in mind, writers can embark on their fast drafting journey with the confidence of a well-prepared athlete before match day and the determination of a bloodhound tackling a bone.

1

PREPARING YOUR WRITING ENVIRONMENT

When embarking on a fast drafting voyage, it is crucial to prepare yourself for success. This chapter focuses on your actions to prepare for effective and productive writing sessions. You can maximize your focus, creativity, and overall output by creating an optimal writing environment, eliminating distractions, establishing a writing schedule, and choosing the right writing tools.

First and foremost, setting up your writing environment is paramount. Designating a dedicated space that is solely for your writing endeavors can have a profound impact on your concentration and inspiration. By creating a physical and mental separation from daily distractions, you can immerse yourself in your writing process, allowing your creativity to flow freely. So, my fellow writer, embrace the power of separation and let yourself be swept away in the current of your creativity. Create the physical and mental space to immerse yourself in the writing process and witness the magic that unfolds when you let your imagination soar.

Eliminating distractions goes hand in hand with creating a conducive writing environment. It is critical to withdraw from the digital world and mute external distractions in this age of perpetual connectedness. So, dear writer, disconnect from the digital realm, silence the noise of notifications, and create a serene and uninterrupted atmosphere. In this space, your focus will flourish, and the depth of your creativity will know no bounds. Embrace the power of this sacred sanctuary, and watch as your words transcend the ordinary, weaving tales that leave an indelible mark on the hearts and minds of your readers.

A writing schedule is another crucial component of preparing for fast drafting. By establishing a routine and allocating dedicated time for your writing practice, you create a framework for consistent progress. Setting daily or weekly writing goals ensures you have a clear target to work toward, helping you maintain momentum and stay on track.

Lastly, choosing the proper writing tools plays a significant role in supporting your fast drafting process. Whether you prefer the tactile experience of writing by hand or the convenience and speed of digital tools, finding the writing tools that resonate with your preferences can enhance your productivity. You may find the tools that best suit your needs and help you release your creativity by experimenting with different options.

This chapter will delve deeper into these crucial elements: setting up your writing environment, eliminating distractions, creating a schedule, and choosing the right writing tools. By implementing these strategies, you will create an ideal foundation for your fast drafting journey, enabling you to maximize your focus, productivity, and overall writing experience. Like a masterful conductor guiding an orchestra, you will orchestrate the symphony of your words with precision and grace, bringing your story to life in a breathtaking crescendo.

Setting up Your Writing Environment

Setting up a suitable writing environment is crucial for writers to cultivate focus, eliminate distractions, and enhance their creative output. A dedicated writing space free from interruptions fosters a milieu conducive to creativity. A dedicated writing space serves as a physical manifestation of a writer's commitment to their craft. It provides a designated area solely devoted to writing, signaling to the mind that it's time to shift into a creative mindset. Whether it's a separate room, a cozy corner, or a specific desk, having a dedicated space allows writers to create a mental boundary between the outside world and their writing process. This separation helps minimize external distractions and enables writers to immerse themselves fully in their work (Ciara, 2018).

Creating a writing environment that is free from distractions is essential for maintaining focus and concentration. Distractions, such as the constant buzzing of a phone, the lure of social media, or the noise of the surrounding environment, can significantly disrupt the writing flow and hinder productivity. You could start by turning off phones and other electronic devices, disconnecting from the internet, and finding a quiet space to minimize external disturbances. You can enter a deep concentration by eliminating these distractions, enabling your creativity to flourish. Furthermore, a conducive writing environment plays a vital role in fostering creativity. You can enhance your creative output by surrounding yourself with elements that inspire and stimulate your imagination. This can be achieved through personalized decor, such as inspirational quotes, artwork, or symbolic objects. Creating an environment that reflects your unique tastes and interests can fuel creativity and provide comfort and inspiration.

Additionally, the physical aspect of the writing environment should be considered. A comfortable chair, a well-organized workspace, and proper lighting create a relaxed and visually pleasing atmosphere. A clutter-free and organized workspace can promote a clear mind and facilitate the free flow of ideas. Setting up a writing space that is free from distractions and conducive to ingenuity is essential for novelists. It provides a dedicated space for writing, minimizes external disturbances, and nurtures inspiration (Ciara, 2018). By creating an environment that supports your writing process, you can enter a focused and creative state, allowing your ideas to flow freely. Your words dance across the page like graceful ballerinas, each step purposeful and exquisite as you produce your best work with an artistry that knows no bounds.

Eliminating Distractions

Eliminating distractions is critical to creating an optimal writing environment and maximizing productivity. Disconnecting from the internet and turning off your phone when writing are two good ways to reduce interruptions. The constant influx of notifications, messages, and alerts from our smartphones can be a significant source of distraction. Every ping or vibration diverts our attention and disrupts the writing flow. By turning off the phone or putting it on silent mode and placing it out of sight, writers can eliminate the temptation to check notifications or engage in unrelated activities.

Similarly, while a valuable resource for research and information, the internet can be a significant distraction. With social media platforms, news websites, and various online entertainment options just a click away, it's easy to get sidetracked and lose valuable writing time. Disconnecting from the internet or using website-blocking applications can help maintain focus and prevent the temptation to engage in online activities unrelated to writing.

By intentionally removing these external distractions, writers can create a focused, uninterrupted writing session. The absence of constant notifications and the allure of internet browsing allow writers to immerse themselves fully in their writing, promoting concentration and productivity. Eliminating distractions enhances focus and enables writers to enter a state of flow. Flow is a mental state characterized by deep engagement and immersion in an activity, where time seems to fly by, and creativity is at its peak (Tracy, 2022). By eliminating distractions, writers can more easily enter this flow state where ideas flow effortlessly, and the writing process becomes more enjoyable and rewarding.

Moreover, eliminating distractions promotes a sense of discipline and commitment to the writing process. By consciously disconnecting from external sources of interruption, writers demonstrate their dedication to their craft and prioritize their writing time. This commitment helps build a habit of focused writing and strengthens the writer's ability to maintain concentration despite potential distractions. Turning off your phone and disconnecting from the internet are effective strategies for eliminating distractions during the writing process. By doing so, writers can create an environment that supports deep focus and concentration, allowing them to fully engage with their writing and unlock their creative potential. Embracing these practices cultivates discipline, promotes the flow state, and enables writers to make the most of their writing sessions.

Creating a Writing Schedule

Creating a writing schedule is like tending to a garden, carefully planting seeds of time and nurturing them with consistency, discipline, and dedication. Setting daily writing goals and scheduling regular writing time establishes a framework that keeps you on track and facilitates consistent progress in your work. These goals can be based on word count, the number of pages, or even the completion of specific scenes or chapters. You can maintain a sense of direction and purpose by breaking the immense writing task into smaller, manageable goals. These goals serve as milestones, allowing you to measure your progress and celebrate your achievements.

In addition to setting goals, scheduling regular writing time is essential for building a writing routine. Consistency is crucial in sharpening writing skills and making progress on a project. You establish a disciplined approach and regularly engage with your craft by dedicating specific time slots to writing. Whether it's early morning, late at night, or during designated breaks, finding a time that works best for your schedule ensures that writing becomes a prioritized and integrated part of your daily routine.

A writing schedule provides structure and accountability. By treating writing time as a commitment, writers are less likely to make excuses or allow other tasks to take precedence. It helps establish boundaries with other responsibilities and obligations, ensuring that writing is given the attention it deserves. Furthermore, having a consistent writing schedule helps writers overcome resistance and creative blocks. When writing becomes a regular practice, the mind attests to the writing process, making it easier to get into the flow and generate ideas. A well-designed writing schedule allows flexibility and adaptability. Life is unpredictable, and circumstances may occasionally disrupt the established routine. However, having a schedule will enable writers to adjust and find alternative time slots while maintaining their progress. It provides a framework that can be modified to accommodate unexpected events or changes in daily routines.

Creating a writing schedule by setting daily goals and scheduling regular writing time is an effective strategy for staying on track and making consistent progress. By breaking down the writing task into manageable goals and allocating dedicated time for writing, writers establish a disciplined routine, develop writing habits, and ensure that their work receives the necessary attention and commitment. Just as a ship's crew maintains a disciplined routine, writers adhere to their scheduled writing sessions with unwavering dedication. They hoist the sails of inspiration, catching the winds of motivation to propel their words forward. Each scheduled session becomes a sacred ritual when they step onto the deck of their imagination, ready to embark on a voyage of creation.

Choosing the Correct Writing Tools

Selecting the proper writing tools is a focal factor for novelists, as they can significantly impact their comfort, productivity, and creative process. The choice of writing tools is subjective and varies from author to author. Exploring and experimenting with different options is essential to find what works best for individual preferences and needs. One of the primary considerations in choosing writing tools is the medium: handwritten or digital. Some people find that the tactile experience of writing by hand enhances their connection with the creative process. A sense of closeness may be evoked, and thoughts can flow more easily when pen meets paper. Handwriting can also offer a slower pace, giving writers time to think and reflect as they compose their ideas.

On the other hand, many artists opt for digital tools such as computers, laptops, or tablets. Digital writing tools provide convenience, ease of editing, and the ability to revise and rearrange text quickly. Word processing software allows one to easily make changes, copy and paste sections, and utilize various formatting options. Additionally, digital tools offer the advantage of automatic spell-checking, word count tracking, and the ability to back up work digitally, minimizing the risk of losing progress. Beyond the medium, the choice of specific writing tools depends on individual preferences. Some writers may prefer using traditional notebooks, journals, or specialized writing pads. These physical tools can offer a sense of nostalgia and a break from digital distractions. Others may opt for specific types of pens or pencils that feel comfortable and smooth to write with or even utilize specialized writing instruments like fountain pens to add a touch of elegance to their process.

A wide range of writing software and applications is available for those who prefer digital tools. From basic text editors to comprehensive writing software with advanced features, writers can choose what suits their needs and preferences. Some software options offer a distraction-free writing atmosphere, customizable layouts, and organizational features to enhance productivity. Consequently, the aim is to find writing tools that synchronize with your preferences, promote comfort, and facilitate innovation. There is no one-size-fits-all panacea, and what may ignite an inferno of inspiration in one writer's soul may leave another feeling uninspired. The key is to explore various options, experiment with various tools, and assess how they contribute to productivity, inspiration, and the overall writing experience.

Choosing the appropriate writing tools is a personal decision that can significantly impact a writer's comfort and productivity. Whether it's the medium of handwriting or digital writing and the specific tools within those mediums, the focus should be on finding what feels most natural and effective. By exploring different options and experimenting with various writing tools, writers can discover the tools that best support their creative process and enable them to produce their best work. Armed with their chosen tools, writers embark on their creative journeys, embracing the dance of experimentation and discovery. They confidently wield their pens or keyboards, infusing their work with the essence of their authentic selves. With each lexical instrument, they unlock the door to their inner worlds, giving birth to literary works that captivate and inspire audiences.

Key Takeaways

Creating a dedicated and inspiring writing space is essential for maintaining focus and fostering creativity. Designate a specific area free from distractions where you can immerse yourself in your writing process. Minimizing distractions is crucial for staying focused during fast drafting. Turn off your phone, disconnect from the internet, and create a quiet and uninterrupted atmosphere to allow your creativity to flourish. Establishing a writing schedule helps you make consistent progress. Set daily or weekly writing goals and dedicate time to your writing practice. This disciplined approach will help you develop a writing routine and maintain momentum. Find the writing tools that suit your preferences and enhance your productivity. Whether you prefer writing by hand or digital tools, experiment with different options to discover what works best for you and supports your fast drafting process.

By setting up an optimal writing environment, eliminating distractions, creating a writing schedule, and selecting the right writing tools, you lay the groundwork for a successful fast drafting experience. These fundamental elements contribute to your focus, productivity, and all-out writing enjoyment. Embrace these practices to optimize your writing process and unleash your creativity during the fast drafting phase. With each practice you embrace, you become a master cultivator, sowing the seeds of structure, focus, and dedication. Just as a gardener carefully plans the layout of their garden, you create a blueprint for your writing process, mapping out the paths and beds where your art will take root and flourish.

2

BRAINSTORMING AND OUTLINING FOR SPEED

A more epic adventure than the most daring expeditions known to humankind is weaving a fascinating and spellbinding tale. The mission is not for the faint-hearted but for those who possess the strength of a thousand titans. Every word, every sentence, becomes a universe unto itself, exploding with the force of a supernova and expanding the boundaries of imagination. It begins with effective brainstorming, where artists engage in free-flowing thinking to generate various ideas and explore different perspectives. One can uncover unique connections and possibilities that lay the foundation for a robust story idea by embracing non-linear thinking and utilizing techniques like mind mapping. Brainstorming can be done individually or collaboratively, allowing for fresh perspectives and the enhancement of originality.

Once the ideas have been spawned, the next step is to draw up a detailed outline. An outline serves as a roadmap for the narrative, providing structure and coherence to the writer's thoughts and ideas. It helps convey the story clearly to others and ensures consistency and continuity throughout the writing process. By outlining the plot, character arcs, and major story beats, writers can identify weaknesses, gaps, or inconsistencies early on and address them before delving into the actual drafting stage. Outlining techniques can vary depending on the author's inclinations and writing styles. Traditional hierarchical outlines break down the story into sections, chapters, scenes, or plot points, establishing a logical order and progression of ideas. Visual outlines, such as storyboards or mind maps, offer a visual representation of the story's structure, facilitating the identification of gaps or pacing issues. Striking a balance between a detailed outline and flexibility allows for organic growth, improvisation, and spontaneous ideas during the writing process.

Staying on track during fast drafting is crucial for maintaining momentum and consistently progressing. Setting daily writing goals, establishing a writing schedule, creating a conducive writing milieu, and utilizing accountability measures can help you stay focused and committed to your writing targets. Flexibility and adaptability are also vital in navigating unforeseen challenges and maintaining consistency in the writing routine. By incorporating effective brainstorming techniques, creating a detailed outline, utilizing outlining techniques, and implementing strategies to stay on track, writers can lay a solid foundation for their fast drafting process. These fundamental elements are guardians of creativity, bestowing artists the gifts of structure, organization, and focus. They are like ancient pillars, standing tall and strong, supporting the weight of imagination and breathing life into stagnant storylines.

Developing a Strong Story

When brainstorming, the objective is to think freely and generate multiple ideas that cover the chosen topic in-depth. This creative technique lets authors explore various angles, perspectives, and possibilities, ultimately developing a solid story idea. During brainstorming, writers are encouraged to think outside the box and embrace a non-linear approach to idea generation. This allows for a more expansive exploration of the chosen theme, plot, characters, or setting. Free-flowing thinking can uncover unique and unexpected connections, sparking creativity and generating fresh narrative concepts.

Brainstorming sessions can take various forms depending on the individual. Some authors may prefer solo brainstorming, retreating to a quiet space, and jotting down ideas stream-of-consciousness (MasterClass, 2021d). Others may opt for group brainstorming, collaborating with fellow artists to bounce ideas off each other and stimulate new perspectives. Furthermore, brainstorming can be enhanced by employing various techniques and tools. Mind mapping, for example, allows writers to organize their thoughts and connect different story elements visually. This technique aids in identifying relationships between characters, plot points, and themes, leading to a more cohesive story idea.

The pivotal benefit of brainstorming lies in its ability to foster creativity and encourage expansive thinking. By exploring ideas both deeply and widely, writers can tap into their vast and unexplored oceans of imagination and uncover unique literary elements that have the potential to enthrall readers. Brainstorming provides a fertile ground for inspiration, allowing artists to overcome creative blocks and generate compelling novels. Developing a solid story idea begins with effective brainstorming (MasterClass, 2021d). By employing techniques that encourage free thinking and exploring various perspectives, writers can delve deeply into their chosen topic, uncovering unique connections and generating fresh storylines. Embracing brainstorming as a creative tool empowers artists to think beyond the conventional, ultimately constructing compelling and engaging story ideas that form the concrete foundation of a successful fast drafting process.

Creating an Outline

A detailed outline helps organize and structure the writer's thoughts and ideas. Outlining serves as a framework that brings clarity to the writer and enables them to convey their stories distinctly to readers. When it comes to outlining, the primary objective is to provide a blueprint for the narrative. It involves breaking down the story into essential components, such as the plot, subplots, character arcs, and major story beats. By delineating these elements, the writer comprehensively understands the story's structure and progression. An outline is a guiding light that ensures coherence and consistency throughout the writing process (How to Outline a Story, n.d.). It helps writers keep track of essential details, maintain continuity, and avoid plot holes or inconsistencies. Additionally, outlining allows writers to identify any potential weaknesses or gaps in the story early on, allowing them to address these issues before delving into the writing process.

One of the main advantages of crafting a detailed outline is the ability to communicate the story effectively to others. With a well-structured framework, writers can clearly articulate their story's central concepts, plot points, and character arcs to editors, beta readers, or collaborators. This crystal-clear communication aids in receiving valuable feedback and ensuring that the intended message of the story is effectively communicated. Outlining techniques may vary depending on the writer. Some writers prefer a traditional linear outline, while others may opt for a more visual approach, such as a storyboard or a mind map.

The chosen outlining method should resonate with the writer's needs and provide a clear and organized structure to work with. A detailed outline is a valuable tool that helps writers organize their thoughts and provide a clear framework for their stories. It allows for clear communication clarity and ensures coherence and consistency throughout the writing process. By outlining the plot, character arcs, and major story beats, writers can effectively convey their ideas to others and receive valuable feedback. Embracing the practice of outlining sets the stage for a well-structured and focused fast drafting experience.

Outlining Techniques

Outlining techniques play a vital role in the fast drafting process by providing a structure and logical order to the writer's content. Outlining comes after the brainstorming phase and is essential for organizing and structuring the writer's ideas. During the outlining phase, writers transform the raw material generated during brainstorming into a coherent and well-organized framework. Imagine this goal as a celestial cartographer, painting constellations across the writer's mind. It orchestrates the celestial bodies of plot points, characters, and settings, aligning them in perfect harmony. Each scene becomes a star, shining brightly in the vast expanse of the narrative, guiding the reader's gaze and leading them deeper into the writer's world.

One commonly used outlining technique is the traditional hierarchical outline (How to Outline a Story, n.d.). In this approach, writers break down their stories into sections, chapters, scenes, or key plot points. They establish a hierarchical structure that allows for a clear progression of ideas and events. Writers can use bullet points, numbering, or any other visual markers to denote the different hierarchy levels within the outline. Another outlining technique is the storyboard or visual outline. Particularly useful for visual thinkers, this approach involves creating a visual representation of the story's structure. Writers can use index cards, sticky notes, or digital tools to represent different scenes or plot points and arrange them on a board or digital canvas. This technique provides:

- A visual overview of the story
- Allowing writers to quickly identify gaps
- Pacing issues
- Areas that require further development

For fast drafting, it's essential to strike a balance between a detailed outline and leaving room for flexibility and creativity. While a comprehensive outline provides a clear game plan, too much rigidity can stifle the creative process. Writers may create a loose outline that provides a general direction while allowing for naturally and spontaneity during the drafting process. The outlining phase also provides for refining and solidifying the story's structure, character arcs, and major plot points (How to Outline a Story, n.d.). Writers can identify any potential weaknesses, inconsistencies, or gaps in the narrative and address them before embarking on the fast drafting process. This helps in maintaining a smooth and uninterrupted flow during the writing stage.

Outlining techniques are essential for fast drafting as they structure and organize the writer's ideas. Through hierarchical outlines or visual storyboards, outlining helps writers establish a logical order and progression of events. It allows for better planning, identifying areas that require further development, and maintaining coherence in the narrative. By finding the best outlining technique, writers can streamline the fast drafting process and confidently embark on their voyage, evoking their story's inner magic.

Tips for Staying on Track

Keeping focused during the fast drafting is crucial to maintaining momentum and consistently progressing. Several tips can help writers stay focused and committed to their writing goals. One practical tip is to set daily writing goals. By establishing specific targets for each writing session, writers create a sense of purpose and direction. These goals can be based on word count, page count, or completing a specific scene or chapter. Breaking down the writing task into smaller, manageable goals provides a clear guideline for day-to-day progress. Creating a writing schedule is another valuable tip for staying on track (Tracy, 2022). Authors establish a routine and a habit of consistent productivity by allocating dedicated and regular time slots for writing. This may be achieved by choosing the times of day when writing is most fruitful and designating those hours specifically for writing tasks. Whether it's early mornings, late evenings, or specific hours, having a designated time for writing helps writers prioritize their craft and make it a consistent part of their daily routine.

Additionally, establishing a conducive writing workspace can significantly contribute to staying focused. Finding a quiet and comfortable spot free from distractions allows writers to focus solely on their writing. This can involve creating a dedicated writing office, minimizing interruptions, and turning off notifications or distractions like phones or internet access. By cultivating an environment that promotes concentration and creativity, writers can immerse themselves fully in the writing process and stay on track. Accountability measures can also help one stay on track. This can involve sharing writing goals or progress with a writing buddy, joining writing groups or communities, or participating in writing challenges. The support and encouragement from others who share similar goals can foster motivation and provide a sense of accountability, ensuring that writers stay committed to their writing schedule and goals.

Lastly, writers need to be flexible and adaptable (Tracy, 2022). While setting goals and establishing a schedule is valuable, it's also essential to recognize that life happens and unforeseen circumstances may disrupt the writing routine. Being open to adjusting schedules, adapting to changes, and forgiving yourself when things don't go as planned can help you navigate challenges and stay on track in the long run. Maintaining focus during the fast drafting process requires setting daily writing goals, establishing a writing schedule, creating a conducive writing environment, and finding accountability measures. By embracing these sacred secrets, writers can summon unwavering focus, orchestrate a symphony of unrelenting progress, and ascend to the glorious summit of their fast-drafting dreams.

Key Takeaways

Brainstorming is a powerful device that allows writers to generate many ideas and explore different perspectives, developing a solid story idea. Embrace non-linear thinking and employ techniques like mind mapping to uncover unique connections and possibilities. Creating a detailed outline serves as a roadmap for the narrative, providing structure and coherence to the writer's thoughts and ideas. It helps convey the story clearly to others, maintains continuity, and identifies weaknesses or inconsistencies early on. Outlining techniques, such as hierarchical outlines and visual storyboards, offer different approaches to organizing and structuring the writer's content. Find the outlining method that resonates with your needs and allows for flexibility and organic growth.

Staying on track during the fast drafting process requires setting daily writing goals, establishing a writing schedule, creating a conducive writing environment, and utilizing accountability measures. Strike a balance between structure and flexibility, adapting to unforeseen challenges while maintaining consistency. Embrace these practices to optimize your writing process and unleash your creativity during the fast drafting phase. Let brainstorming, outlining, staying on track, and flexibility guide your journey toward producing your best work. Crafting a fascinating tale is not a mere expedition but a grand odyssey requiring strength and creativity beyond measure. So, embark on this epic quest, armed with these sacred secrets, and let your artistic works ignite the literary universe of imagination.

3

QUICK DRAFTING TECHNIQUES

In the world of writing, time is a precious commodity. As writers, we often find ourselves grappling with the desire to bring our ideas to life on the page while also contending with the constraints of busy schedules and looming deadlines. This is where fast drafting techniques rescue us, providing a roadmap to unleash our creativity and propel our stories forward with remarkable speed. Fast drafting is a method that prioritizes momentum and output over perfection and precision, allowing us to draft a story quickly and efficiently. In this chapter, we will explore a range of strategies and approaches that can turbocharge your drafting process, helping you conquer the blank page and embrace the exhilaration of capturing your ideas swiftly and intently. We will delve into the art of free writing, which aims to let your words flow without inhibition, allowing your subconscious mind to unveil unexpected plot twists and characters. We will also uncover the power of outlining, a strategic approach that lets you map out your story's structure before diving into the writing, enabling you to draft with purpose and direction.

Furthermore, we will explore techniques such as word sprints; timed writing sessions, where you challenge yourself to write as much as possible in a set amount of time; and writing in bursts, where you focus intensely for short periods, followed by brief breaks to recharge your creative energy. By incorporating these fast drafting techniques into your writing process, you can break through the barriers of self-doubt and perfectionism while harnessing the sheer joy of uninhibited storytelling. Whether you're a seasoned writer seeking to meet tight deadlines or a beginner eager to unlock your creative potential, this chapter will equip you with the tools and mindset needed to embrace fast drafting and unleash your storytelling prowess like never before. Brace yourself and prepare to embark on an exhilarating journey of swift and productive drafting, where your imagination takes flight and your words flow effortlessly onto the page.

Strategies for Writing Quickly

Writing sluggishly can be a formidable challenge for any writer, but fear not! Whether you aim to complete your project promptly, increase your book output, or save time, these ingenious tricks and strategies will help you write faster and more efficiently.

1. Create a writing environment free from distractions. Find a quiet space, turn off notifications, and remove any temptations that may divert your attention. By immersing yourself in a focused and distraction-free zone, you can fully engage with your writing and boost your productivity.
2. Set a stopwatch and encourage yourself to draft as many words as possible in an allotted time. Word sprints create a sense of urgency and can unleash a burst of creativity. The goal is to write without pausing or editing, allowing your thoughts to flow freely. This technique

promotes quick and uninhibited writing, propelling your progress forward.

3. Adopt the Pomodoro Technique. The Pomodoro Technique is a time management method that works in focused intervals. Set a stopwatch for 25 minutes, and dedicate that time solely to writing. After each interval, take a short break before diving into another focused writing session. This structured approach enhances concentration and helps you maintain a steady writing rhythm.
4. Break down your writing tasks into smaller, manageable goals. You create a sense of accomplishment and motivation by setting achievable targets, such as completing a specific word count or a chapter. Reward yourself after reaching each milestone, whether with a small treat, a short break, or a moment of relaxation. These rewards act as incentives and fuel your determination to write faster.
5. Do not slow down. Keep from slowing down when you encounter a challenging section or need to research specific details. Instead, use placeholders. Insert a

temporary note or symbol to indicate where additional information or further development is required, and continue writing without interruption. This technique lets you maintain your writing flow and momentum while tackling challenging aspects later in editing.

6. Boost your writing speed by disconnecting from your screen. Try closing your eyes or minimizing the document window, and focus solely on the keyboard and your thoughts. By eliminating the distractions of visually monitoring your words, you can tap into a deeper level of concentration and let your ideas flow unhindered.
7. Use Technology. Leverage the power of technology by using speech-to-text dictation software or apps. Instead of typing, speak your thoughts aloud while the software transcribes your words. This method allows you to capture ideas quickly and naturally, bypassing the potential slowdown of typing. Speech-to-text dictation can be especially beneficial during brainstorming sessions or when

you want to grab a rapid stream of consciousness.

8. Visualize before you write. Before you start writing a scene or chapter, please take a moment to visualize it in your mind. Imagine the setting, the characters, the actions, and the emotions involved. By mentally rehearsing the scene beforehand, you'll have clarity of what you intend to convey, making it easier to translate your thinking into words when you write. This visualization technique saves time by reducing pauses and uncertainties during the writing process (Reedsy Team, 2022).

Incorporating these eight strategies into your writing routine will help you overcome the hurdles of slow writing and supercharge your productivity. Remember, the key is to find the techniques that resonate with your imagination and adapt them to your unique writing style. With determination, focus, and a few clever tricks, you'll be amazed at how much quicker and more efficiently you can bring your ideas to life on the page.

Overcoming Writer's Block

Regardless of your writing location, make it where you feel comfortable and motivated. Declutter the space and add inspiring elements, such as fresh flowers or a picture with special meaning. By personalizing your workspace, you create an environment that encourages creativity and focus.

The Pomodoro Technique, developed by Francesco Cirillo, promotes focused work in 25-minute intervals, known as Pomodoros, followed by short breaks (Tracy, 2022). Set a stopwatch on your phone or use a productivity app to stay on track. During each Pomodoro, eliminate distractions like checking emails or getting up for unnecessary tasks. Once the timer goes off, take a well-deserved break to recharge. This technique helps maintain concentration and increases productivity.

Overcoming writer's block often requires discipline and consistency. Take inspiration from successful authors like John Grisham, who have established a successful writing routine (Tracy, 2022). Choose a specific time to write and commit to it. Even if you don't feel inspired or have ideas immediately, showing up and dedicating yourself to writing can break through resistance and foster creativity.

Like the writing exercises of your school days, use writing prompts to kick start your writing session. Writer's Digest provides a section on its website dedicated to prompts (Tracy, 2022). Set aside dedicated time to write based on these prompts. They can help you overcome the initial hurdle of getting started and unlock your creative flow.

Striving for a flawless first draft can hinder your progress and lead to writer's paralysis. Instead, focus on the process rather than perfection. Don't worry about spelling, grammar, or producing polished writing during the initial drafting stage. Just let your thoughts flow and get them down on paper. You can always revise and edit later. Using filler words or phrases can help you articulate your ideas more easily. These can be refined during the editing phase.

Reading is an outstanding source of inspiration for writers. Engage with literature or other written works before starting your writing session. Spend a few minutes reading poetry, a chapter from a book, or a short essay (Tracy, 2022). This activity can stimulate your creative mindset and help you find your writing voice or draw inspiration from your favorite authors.

Rather than giving power to the concept of writer's block, consider the perspective that it is an artificial construct (Tracy, 2022). Psychologists argue that naming it can magnify the problem. Instead, approach writing with determination and perseverance. Refuse to acknowledge writer's block as an obstacle. Sit down at your desk and prove you can overcome challenges through dedication and action.

By enhancing your workspace and implementing these strategies, you can create an environment that fosters productivity and creativity, helping you write more quickly and efficiently. "Ah, writer's block," you declare, your words resonating confidently. "You may taunt and tease, but I refuse to be trapped by your illusory grip. You are a mere construct, a figment of doubt that seeks to thwart my progress. I see through your deceptive veil and reclaim the power of my imagination."

Using Prompts and Exercises

Whether you're suffering from writer's block or want to shake things up, here are some free writing prompts to ensure you make the most of your writing time. Think of them as story starters or warm-ups to get the creative juices flowing. Furthermore, remember that free writing aims to get you to start writing—not to produce publishable work. So, when you sit down to try some of these story ideas, remind yourself that everything you write is just for fun; it shouldn't be hard work and won't be part of your next fiction writing project (MasterClass, 2021a).

1. Think of an occasion where you were terrified, and put a character in that situation.
2. Write about a seventy-year-old woman who has lived her whole life in a dystopian society but has survived long enough that things are becoming stable again.
3. Pick one of your favorite books and rewrite the conflict of the first scene using your characters.
4. Write a scene in which all the character development comes from dialogue—no descriptions of how a character feels or what they're doing.

5. Write a one-paragraph ghost story thriller —but set somewhere surprising, like a beach resort or Mars.
6. Write a scene about a woman who discovers a close family member has just robbed a bank. Describe how she reacts to hearing the news for the first time.
7. Draft a story about a man who loves journaling, but when he sits down one day to write an entry, he sees someone else has already written one for him.
8. Write a scene in a fantasy world where everyone who dies is reincarnated and can remember their past lives.
9. Write about a college student whose favorite place is the local bar because he's friends with the ghost that lives in the toilet stall.
10. Draft a story in which the main character wants so badly to go back to high school that they invent rudimentary time travel to relive the days of their younger self but end up going too far and getting stuck in middle school.
11. Draft a first-person narrative from the point of view of a tree that suddenly has a tree house being built in it.

12. Write a meta-story in which a character is writing a book. Still, they have such a hard time that they decide to enroll in writing classes or join a writing group led by the town's arrogant and infamous local horror writer.
13. Choose random words from the dictionary and use them in your story's first line.

These prompts are designed to spark your creativity and encourage you to explore new ideas. Use them as a starting point to let your imagination run wild and see where your writing takes you. Remember, the most essential thing is to have fun and enjoy the process of writing (MasterClass, 2021a).

Maintaining Consistency and Momentum

Writing a novel is a creative endeavor that requires dedication, organization, and discipline. To embark on this adventure and see it through to the end, it's essential to develop good habits and strategies that will help you maintain consistency and momentum in your writing process. Time management is crucial when writing a novel. Determine specific periods in your schedule that are dedicated solely to writing. This could be a couple of hours every day, or longer stretches on certain days of the week. By setting aside consistent blocks of time, you create a routine and establish a writing habit.

When you have limited writing time, making the most of it becomes even more important. Prioritize your writing tasks and focus on the most critical aspects of your novel. This might include working on key scenes, developing crucial plot points, or fine-tuning character arcs. Avoid distractions during your writing sessions and stay focused on the task. Having a routine can be immensely helpful in maintaining consistency. Set a specific time and place for writing, and stick to it as much as possible. By making writing a regular part of your day, you condition your mind to be creative during those dedicated times, making it easier to dive into your story.

Break down your novel-writing process into smaller, achievable goals. Each day, set specific targets for the amount of writing you aim to accomplish. This could be a word count goal or completing a particular scene or chapter. By setting daily goals, you create a sense of progress and accomplishment, which can motivate you to keep going. Familiarize yourself with the genre in which you're writing. Read widely within that genre and study successful authors' techniques and storytelling approaches. Please consider how they develop their characters, build tension, and create immersive worlds. This study will help you understand the expectations and conventions of your genre, allowing you to better craft your novel. Characters are the heart and soul of a novel. Spend time developing your main characters before diving into writing. Understand their backstories, motivations, and desires. Create character profiles, and get to know them intimately. This will help you bring depth and complexity to your characters, making them relatable and engaging for your readers.

By incorporating these strategies into your novel-writing process, you can enhance consistency and maintain the momentum needed to see your project through to completion. Remember, writing a novel is a journey, and developing good habits and disciplined approaches will contribute to your success as an author. This journey is not without its challenges, but with dedication and discipline, you can transform words into magic. Embrace the power of habit, navigate the unpredictable terrain with resilience, and infuse your writing with the vivid imagery of the world around you. As you journey forth, may your pen dance across the pages, weaving tales that captivate hearts and leave an indelible mark on the literary landscape.

Key Takeaways

Creating a dedicated writing environment is essential for minimizing distractions and focusing on your work. Locate a peaceful and comfortable location where you can work uninterrupted and remove potential distractions like phones or other devices. A dedicated space helps signal to your brain that it's time to focus, making it easier to get into a flow state. Personalize your environment with inspiring items and engage your senses to make it a motivating space. Try word sprints and the Pomodoro Technique to increase productivity and tap into your creativity. Word sprints involve setting a timer and writing as much as feasible in a short time, encouraging a continuous flow of ideas. The Pomodoro Technique consists in working in focused intervals followed by short breaks, allowing you to stay engaged and productive while providing opportunities for rest.

Setting small goals and using placeholders can motivate and keep your writing momentum. Break down your writing tasks into achievable milestones, and reward yourself when you accomplish them. Use placeholders for challenging sections or when research is needed to maintain the flow of your writing. Visualizing scenes before writing them and using speech-to-text dictation tools can also enhance your writing process and capture ideas efficiently. Establishing a writing routine with consistent blocks of time and prioritizing tasks helps build discipline and maintain focus. Treat your writing time as sacred and commit to it. Minimize distractions, manage your time effectively, and dedicate specific times and places for writing to condition your mind for creativity. Studying books in your genre and developing well-rounded characters also contribute to improving your writing skills and creating engaging stories.

By incorporating these strategies and techniques into your writing process, you can overcome challenges, increase productivity, and maintain consistency. Explore various ways to see what works most efficiently for you, and embrace the joy of writing. Stay committed to your craft, and your writing will flourish.

4

DEVELOPING COMPELLING CHARACTERS

Creating realistic and compelling characters is fundamental to crafting engaging and immersive stories. While it's common for characters to appear flat or two-dimensional initially, they should evolve into individuals with desires, fears, and complexities. Instead of plot devices, they should be individuals to whom the story happens. In this guide, we will explore key takeaways to assist you in bringing your characters to life and making them captivating and relatable to readers.

To develop well-rounded characters, drawing inspiration from real people can be invaluable. Along your literary voyage, remember those who have made an indelible imprint on you in the past. Allow their presence to guide your pen, infusing your words with the echoes of their voices and the echoes of your shared experiences. They could be your family members, friends, acquaintances, or even strangers whose paths briefly intertwined with yours.

Reflect on the moments, conversations, or gestures that made them stand out, imprinting your heart and mind. Use their unique traits, personalities, and relationships as a starting point for crafting your characters. You can create more vivid and authentic portrayals by infusing your characters with the qualities you observe in real people.

Understanding the emotional triggers that have shaped your life is another powerful tool for character development. Reflect on your moments of fear, courage, sorrow, joy, failure, shame, guilt, and forgiveness. These experiences provide insights into your characters' vulnerabilities, desires, and contradictions. You can create more compelling and relatable portrayals by exploring similar emotional incidents in your characters' lives.

Once you have identified the emotional triggers, it's essential to envision specific scenes from your characters' lives. Imagine moments that reveal their vulnerabilities, desires, and contradictions. By visualizing these scenes, you gain a clearer understanding of your characters as distinct entities capable of acting on their own. This process enables you to render them more vividly on the page, making them come alive for readers.

Developing character profiles is another valuable technique for creating well-rounded characters. Envision your characters' entire life journeys, from birth to death. Consider their motivations, preferences, hobbies, and past experiences. Although not all of these details may explicitly appear in your writing, they shape your characters' identities and influence their actions, making them more believable and relatable to readers.

Integrating character arcs into your story is a crucial aspect of character development. Character arcs trace the growth and transformation of your protagonist throughout the narrative. Identify their flaws or weaknesses, and set up events that challenge them. Allow your characters to learn, evolve, and overcome their shortcomings, resulting in a personal transformation that aligns with the themes and objectives of your story.

Finally, it's essential to avoid common character pitfalls that detract from their believability and impact. Steer clear of relying on stereotypes and clichés, creating unrealistic or unlikable characters, and falling into predictable character arcs. Instead, strive for uniqueness, authenticity, and complexity in your characters. Give them depth through rich backstories, detailed descriptions, a range of emotions, clear motivations, and a balance of strengths and flaws.

Developing Realistic and Compelling Characters

When creating characters for our stories, it is common for them to initially appear flat or two-dimensional. They serve the purpose of filling a role in the plot rather than being independent beings with desires, fears, and complexities. Compelling characters are not simply meager plot devices; they are individuals and living human beings to whom the story happens. While some stories begin with characters and their needs driving the narrative, many mainstream and genre fiction works start with a story idea, requiring the characters to be fleshed out to avoid being stock players in the drama. In bringing your characters to life, you become a creator, a conjurer of souls, infusing them with a vitality that resonates beyond the pages of your story. This feat requires superior levels of talent and insight, despite the perception that genre fiction is an inferior art form. So, how do we flesh out our characters when they emerge from story needs or lack specificity and power? The best inspiration often comes from within us and our experiences with real people.

Start by reflecting on the following individuals:

- A family member you feel particularly close to
- A family member you particularly dislike or are estranged from
- Childhood friends, both you've lost touch with and those you're still in contact with
- Strangers you've encountered recently
- People you know personally and admire or fear
- Past and present loves, both the ones who got away and the ones you wished had
- Childhood and adulthood nemeses
- Annoying individuals from the past and present
- Favorite and least favorite neighbors and co-workers
- People you interact with daily on a business level
- Those who have inspired or believed in you and those who have doubted you

- Individuals you harbor secret crushes on or feel attracted to
- People you believe have crushes on you

This list can be expanded based on inventiveness (Corbett, 2011). Writing down these characters provides a more extensive cast than you might have initially realized. Sometimes, we repeatedly fall into patterns of writing variations of the same character. Using individuals, we know as inspiration allows us to see them vividly and precisely, giving a unique real-life feel to our characters. However, real people are only some of the perfect source material. We must also draw on our lives to understand a character's inner world. Explore the emotional triggers in your own life and those of your characters.

These include:

- Your moment of greatest fear
- Your moment of greatest courage
- Your moment of greatest sorrow
- Your moment of greatest joy
- Your worst failure
- Your moment of deepest shame
- Your moment of most profound guilt

- Your moment of most redemptive forgiveness

By reflecting on these emotional incidents, you gain insights into your characters' vulnerabilities, secrets, desires, and contradictions (Corbett, 2011). These moments serve as yardsticks and access points to explore similar experiences in the lives of your characters, allowing for more compelling portrayals. The trick is to envision these scenes in your characters' experiences after exploring them on your own. As you delve into their emotional journeys, you will gain a clearer image of your characters, enabling you to render them on the page. Once you can see them as distinct entities capable of acting independently, you can engage in a dialogue with them, asking the crucial questions that form the foundation of your story.

Creating Character Profiles

Characterization and character development are indeed the more intricate aspects of writing. To create a believable character, imagining their entire life journey from the cradle to the grave is essential. While this may seem overwhelming, a deep understanding of the character is crucial for portraying their responses and actions. Knowing their thoughts, dialogue, and behaviors allows you to make informed decisions when placing them in various situations. Understanding a character's motivations, preferences, and hobbies is particularly important in character-driven historical fiction. These details contribute to creating a realistic and relatable character for readers. Even if you don't explicitly explore a character's entire life in your writing, their past experiences shape who they are in the present and influence their future actions. One effective way to develop a better understanding of character creation is to analyze memorable characters from the works of professional authors. Take a few moments to reflect on what makes these characters memorable and note your observations for future reference. Several narrative devices help bring characters to life.

Pay attention to how your character speaks. Do they use long-winded sentences or prefer concise expressions? How they respond or hold back during arguments reveals their personality. Study the dialogue of authors you admire to see how they create believable and revealing conversations. Consider how your character engages with the world around them. Are they passive or active? Their interactions with situations, other characters, and the environment reflect their core identity. Reflect on your interactions in everyday life to draw inspiration for your character's behavior. What your character does, or doesn't do, propels the plot forward. Their actions determine whether they are a hero or a reluctant hero in the quest you've set for them. Ensure that your character's actions align with their motivations and personality traits. A character's intrinsic nature, like Lisbeth Salander in The Girl with the Dragon Tattoo (Larsson, 2005), contributes to their memorability (Jenkins, 2022). This nature is often revealed through their backstory. Consider how your character's nature influences their actions, interactions, and speech, making them distinctive and memorable. Imperfections make characters more relatable and believable. Just as no person in real life is without flaws; your character should have their own set of shortcomings. Embrace these flaws, as they add depth and complexity to your character, resonating with readers.

Strong characterization stems from the deep knowledge of your protagonist. The more you know about them, the better you can portray them. This knowledge will naturally find its way into your writing, enhancing the authenticity of your character. Conversely, lacking a deep understanding of your character will limit your ability to develop them fully. Commit time and effort to establish a thorough grasp of your protagonist. Immerse yourself in their world, put yourself in their shoes, and listen to their heart's whispers. As a result, you will produce a character that bounces off the page, enthralling audiences and leaving an unforgettable impression on their minds.

Incorporating Character Arcs Into Your Story

A character arc is a crucial element in storytelling that outlines the transformation and growth of a character throughout the narrative. It traces the protagonist's journey from comfort or stagnation to the point of upheaval or changes, eventually returning to a new state of equilibrium or resolution. By incorporating character arcs into your story, you can create engaging and dynamic characters that resonate with readers. To develop a character arc, you can begin by identifying your protagonist's flaw or weakness. This flaw serves as a starting point for their personal growth and transformation. It could be a character trait, a deeply ingrained belief, a fear, or any other aspect that hinders their progress or fulfillment (Weiland, 2016).

Next, set up an event (or series of events) early in the story that challenges your protagonist and forces them to confront their flaw head-on. This event acts as a catalyst for change and propels the character out of their comfort zone. It creates a sense of conflict or tension that drives the narrative forward. As the story progresses, allow your character to navigate the challenges and obstacles. Along the way, provide opportunities for your protagonist to learn, evolve, and overcome their flaws. This could involve acquiring new skills, gaining insights, forming new relationships, or experiencing significant realizations.

As your character grows and works through their flaws, they should gradually develop new strengths, values, or perspectives. This transformation should be organic and realistic, allowing the readers to witness the character's gradual progression. The protagonist becomes more resilient, empowered, or enlightened by overcoming their flaws. Finally, bring the character arc to a satisfying conclusion by showcasing how the protagonist's growth and newfound strengths enable them to face the story's climax or ultimate challenge. They should utilize the lessons learned and the changes they've undergone to overcome the central conflict.

It is important to note that character arcs can take various forms depending on the story and the character's journey. Some arcs involve a complete transformation, while others may focus on acceptance or finding inner strength. The key is ensuring the character's authentic growth aligns with the narrative's themes and objectives (Weiland, 2016). By incorporating well-crafted character arcs into your story, you can add depth, emotional resonance, and a sense of fulfillment to your characters' journeys. This creates a more engaging reading experience and allows readers to connect with and root for the characters as they navigate their personal evolution.

Avoiding Common Character Pitfalls

When crafting characters for a novel, it's essential to avoid common pitfalls that can detract from their believability and impact. The following are some common character pitfalls to avoid and strategies to overcome them:

- Characters that conform to stereotypes or rely on clichéd traits. This can feel one-dimensional and lacks originality. To avoid this, strive for uniqueness and complexity in your characters. Consider their eccentricities, backgrounds, and experiences that shape who they are. Challenge stereotypes by subverting expectations or giving characters unexpected qualities or motivations.

- Characters that are too perfect or lacking in relatability can alienate readers. Aim for characters that feel authentic and flawed. They should have strengths and weaknesses, virtues and vices, and emotions. Explore their vulnerabilities, insecurities, and struggles to make them relatable and three-dimensional. Additionally, give them qualities readers can admire or sympathize with, even if they aren't likable. Predictability can make characters and their journeys feel stale or unengaging.

Surprise your readers by avoiding overly formulaic character arcs or expected outcomes. Develop characters with complexity and depth, and introduce unexpected twists and turns in their development. Allow them to grow, change, and surprise themselves and the readers.

To overcome these pitfalls and create compelling characters, consider the following strategies:

- Develop a backstory that provides insights into your character's upbringing, experiences, and pivotal moments in their life. This will help shape their personality, beliefs, and motivations. Understanding their past can inform their present actions and decisions, adding depth and richness to their characterization.
- Move beyond surface-level physical descriptions, and delve into your character's mannerisms, gestures, and unique traits. Consider their internal thoughts and perspectives, as well as their external behaviors.
- Use vivid and specific language to bring your characters to life, enabling readers to visualize and connect with them on a deeper level.

Humans are complex beings with many emotions, and your characters should reflect this complexity. Show their joys, fears, sorrows, and triumphs. Explore how they react and evolve emotionally throughout the story. Emphasize their emotional journeys and let readers experience the ups and downs alongside them. Characters should have clear goals and desires that drive their actions. Understand what motivates your characters and why they pursue specific paths. This will make their actions more meaningful and their choices more understandable to readers. Characters with fears and flaws are relatable and human. Explore their insecurities, weaknesses, and internal conflicts (Weiland, 2016). This adds depth to their personalities and creates opportunities for growth and development throughout the story.

While flaws are essential, characters should also possess strengths or positive qualities that make them compelling and admirable. These strengths can help them overcome challenges and contribute to their growth. Balance their flaws with redeeming qualities that readers can appreciate. By avoiding stereotypes, creating realistic and likable characters, and introducing unexpected elements, you can develop engaging and memorable characters that resonate with readers. Remember to explore their origin stories, provide in-depth descriptions, evoke a range of emotions, and establish motivations, and balance fears and flaws with strengths. With careful attention to characterization, your characters will come alive on the pages of your novel.

Key Takeaways

Move beyond flat, two-dimensional characters by treating them as independent beings with desires, fears, and complexities. Avoid using them as plot devices, and make them individuals to whom the story happens. Look to your own experiences and the people you know for inspiration. Reflect on family members, friends, acquaintances, and even strangers who have left an impression on you. Use their traits, personalities, and relationships as a starting point for creating well-rounded characters. Dive into your own life and the emotional incidents that have shaped you. Reflect on moments of fear, courage, sorrow, joy, failure, shame, guilt, and forgiveness. Understanding your vulnerabilities allows you to empathize with your characters and delve into their inner worlds. Once you have identified emotional triggers, imagine similar experiences for your characters. Visualize specific moments that reveal their vulnerabilities, desires, and contradictions. This process helps you understand your characters deeper and renders them more vividly on the page.

Develop a comprehensive understanding of your characters by envisioning their entire life journey from birth to death. Consider their motivations, preferences, hobbies, and past experiences. Even if these details don't explicitly appear in your writing, they shape your characters' identities and influence their actions. Character arcs trace the growth and transformation of your protagonist throughout the story. Identify their flaws or weaknesses and set up events that challenge them. Allow your characters to learn, evolve, and overcome their shortcomings, resulting in a personal transformation that aligns with the narrative's themes and objectives. Steer clear of relying on stereotypes, creating unrealistic or unlikable characters, and being predictable. Strive for uniqueness, authenticity, and complexity in your characters. Give them depth through backstory, detailed descriptions, a range of emotions, clear motivations, and a balance of strengths and flaws. By embracing these practices, you can create compelling and well-rounded characters that resonate with readers, breathe life into your storytelling, and leave an indelible mark on the hearts and minds of your audience.

5

DIALOG AND DESCRIPTION

When it comes to writing dialogue, genuineness is paramount. Realistic conversations mirror natural speech patterns while still serving a purpose. By paying attention to rhythm, tone, and vocabulary, you can ensure that your characters' dialogue reflects their unique personalities and backgrounds. Remember, dialogue should go beyond information exchange; it should show emotions, conflicts, and relationships, allowing characters to reveal their thoughts, feelings, and motivations. This adds depth to their interactions, drawing readers into the story. Dialogue is an effective way to advance the plot. It should propel the story forward by revealing important information, introducing conflicts or obstacles, and contributing to character development. Each conversation should have a purpose, moving the narrative meaningfully. Effective dialogue often contains subtext, where characters imply or hint at something beneath the surface. By incorporating subtext, you add complexity and intrigue to their interactions. This encourages readers to read between the lines and connect with the narrative more fundamentally.

Describing settings and environments is another crucial aspect of storytelling. Weave dialogue into your descriptions to strike the right balance, breaking up long passages and adding variety to the narrative. This approach keeps the reader engaged and provides opportunities for character interactions that reveal their reactions to the surroundings. Purposeful descriptions are essential and should serve a specific function in the story. Whether it's setting the mood, enhancing characterization, advancing the plot, or creating symbolism, avoid excessive or unnecessary details that don't add value to the story. Instead, use descriptions to establish the desired mood or atmosphere, enhancing the reader's emotional experience. You can also strengthen characterization through skillful descriptions by showing how characters interact with and respond to their surroundings. This reveals aspects of their personality, motivations, or conflicts, deepening the reader's understanding and connection.

Furthermore, descriptions can be instrumental in advancing the plot by conveying important information, introducing relevant elements, or foreshadowing future events that drive the story forward. They can also be imbued with symbolism, using settings, buildings, or natural elements to symbolize deeper themes or motifs, adding layers of meaning and depth to your story. To create a vivid and immersive experience, sensory details should be employed. Engage your readers' senses by incorporating descriptive adjectives depicting the setting and characters. But don't stop at visual descriptions alone. Dive deeper into the sensory experience by engaging other senses. Use adjectives that evoke scents to transport your readers to a fragrant garden filled with blooming flowers or a bustling kitchen infused with the aroma of freshly baked bread. Employ adjectives that conjure sounds to immerse your readers in the cacophony of a bustling marketplace or the tranquil melody of a babbling brook.

Capture auditory details through onomatopoeia, descriptive verbs, and comparisons, allowing readers to hear the sounds within your story.

Evoking scents transports readers into your story's universe, tapping into powerful emotions. Including taste sensations deepens the reader's connection by evoking specific flavors and textures. Conveying how something feels to the touch through adjectives and similes engages readers physically in the story. Additionally, literary devices such as metaphors, similes, and other figures of speech can create vivid and evocative descriptions. However, it's essential to exercise selectivity and purpose when choosing sensory details. Focus on those most relevant to the scene, character, or atmosphere, ensuring they contribute to the narrative.

Finally, let's explore tips for improving your writing style. Developing well-rounded and relatable characters is crucial for compelling storytelling. Please pay attention to their backgrounds, motivations, and growth throughout the story, allowing them to evolve and engage readers deeper. Craft a strong plot with purposeful events and conflicts that drive the story forward, keeping readers invested. Incorporate literary devices such as foreshadowing and symbolism to enhance the complexity and impact of your storytelling. Show, don't tell, using vivid descriptions, actions, and dialogue to immerse readers in the story. Experiment with sentence lengths and structures to create rhythm and match the mood and pace of your narrative. Reading widely and analyzing successful authors' writing can provide valuable insights and techniques to incorporate into your style. Throughout the editing process, prioritize clarity and conciseness. Trim unnecessary words and phrases that may hinder the flow of your sensory descriptions. Ensure that each sensory detail serves a purpose, deepening the reader's connection to the story and enriching their understanding of the characters and settings.

Writing Effective Dialog

When writing a novel, effective dialogue is fundamental in engaging readers and bringing your story to life. Dialogue reveals character traits, advances the plot, and creates realistic interactions between characters. Dialogue should mirror natural speech patterns while being purposeful and concise (Pope, 2022). Avoid excessive rambling or overly formal language unless it aligns with a specific character's traits. Please consider your characters' rhythm, tone, and vocabulary, ensuring their dialogue reflects their unique personalities and backgrounds.

Dialogue can effectively show emotions, conflicts, and relationships rather than explicitly stating them. Through conversations, characters can reveal their thoughts, feelings, and motivations, adding depth and authenticity to their interactions. Dialogue should propel the story forward by revealing important information, introducing conflicts or obstacles, and contributing to character development. Each conversation should have a purpose and move the narrative meaningfully. Effective dialogue often contains subtext, where characters imply or hint at something beneath the surface (Pope, 2022). This adds complexity and intrigue to their interactions, inviting readers to read between the lines and engage with the story more deeply.

Describing Settings and Environment

When describing settings and environments in your novel, finding a balance between dialogue and description is essential. Here's a closer look at achieving that balance and making your descriptions purposeful. Including dialogue in your descriptions helps to break up long passages of descriptive text, adds variety to the narrative, and allows for character interaction (Setting the Scene, n.d.). It can also provide insights into characters' reactions to their surroundings, contributing to their development and the holistic atmosphere of the scene. By weaving dialogue into your descriptions, you engage readers with character interactions and give them a deeper understanding of the setting. For example, characters might comment on the beauty of a landscape or express their discomfort in a gloomy building. These conversations can enhance the atmosphere and immerse readers in the story world.

Descriptions should serve a specific purpose in the story and go beyond mere visual representation. They should contribute to your narrative's plot, character development, or theme. Describing settings and environments can help establish a scene's desired mood or atmosphere. For instance, a dark and foreboding description of a haunted house can create a sense of suspense and anticipation, enhancing the audience's emotional experience. How characters interact with and respond to their surroundings can reveal aspects of their personalities, motivations, or conflicts. Use descriptions to show how a character's perception of the setting influences their emotions and actions. For example, a character's fascination with architecture might be reflected in their detailed observations of a grand cathedral. Descriptions can be used to convey important information or introduce elements that are relevant to the story's progression.

For instance, describing a hidden passageway in a castle might foreshadow a crucial plot twist or serve as a means for characters to escape a dangerous situation later on. Consider using descriptions of buildings, scenery, or natural elements to symbolize deeper themes or motifs in your story. For example, a decaying, abandoned building can symbolize the protagonist's struggles. At the same time, a vibrant, blossoming garden can represent hope and renewal.

Remember, descriptions should have a purpose and contribute to the general narrative. Avoid including excessive or unnecessary details that don't add value to the story. Instead, select significant details, evoke emotions, and contribute to the atmosphere, characterization, or plot development (Setting the Scene, n.d.). Finding the right balance between dialogue and description and ensuring that your descriptions have a point in the story can create a vivid and immersive reading experience for your audience. Through their words, artists build bridges between the real and the imaginary, guiding their readers on an unforgettable journey that transcends the boundaries of time and space.

Using Sensory Details to Enhance Your Writing

Including sensory elements in your writing may help you create a vivid and immersive experience for your readers. Engaging their senses enables them to connect more deeply with the story and make it come alive (MasterClass, 2021c). Here are some ways to effectively incorporate sensory details into your writing.

Sight: Describing visual elements can help readers visualize the setting and characters. Use descriptive adjectives to paint a clear picture, allowing readers to see the colors, shapes, and textures in their mind's eye. To illustrate, instead of simply stating that a room is messy, you can describe it as cluttered with clothes strewn across the floor and papers scattered on the desk.

Sound: Incorporating sounds into your writing can add depth and create a more immersive experience. Use onomatopoeia, descriptive verbs, or comparisons to capture the auditory details of a scene. For instance, instead of saying that a door slammed, you can describe it as a thunderous bang reverberating through the hallway.

Smell: Describing scents can evoke powerful emotions and memories. Using descriptive language and comparisons, you can transport readers into your story's world. Whether it's the aroma of freshly baked bread or the pungent smell of a damp forest, these details can enrich the atmosphere and create a more realistic experience.

Taste: Including taste sensations can further engage readers' senses. Whether it's the sweetness of a ripe fruit or the bitterness of a strong cup of coffee, incorporating taste descriptions can provide a deeper connection to the story. Use descriptive language and comparisons to evoke specific flavors and textures.

Touch: Describing textures and tactile sensations allows readers to engage with the story physically. Use adjectives and similes to convey how something feels to the touch. Whether it's the roughness of tree bark or the silky smoothness of a satin dress, these details help readers connect with the physical world of your story.

Incorporating sensory information goes beyond simply listing adjectives. It uses techniques like metaphors, similes, and other figures of speech to create vivid and evocative descriptions (MasterClass, 2021c). By comparing one sensory experience to another, you can add depth and layers to your writing. For example, you can describe the sound of raindrops on a window as a gentle symphony or compare the taste of a ripe strawberry to a burst of sunshine in your mouth. Remember to use sensory details selectively and purposefully. Choose the most relevant information to the scene, character, or atmosphere you're trying to create. By effectively incorporating sensory details, you can immerse your readers in your story and make it a multisensory experience.

Tips for Improving Your Writing Style

Many measures that must be taken to produce a fascinating and engaging tale. Well-developed and relatable characters are paramount to capturing readers' interest. Pay attention to your characters' backgrounds, motivations, and personalities. Give them depth by exploring their past experiences, desires, and fears. Allow them to evolve and grow throughout the story, facing challenges and making choices that shape their development. A well-crafted plot keeps readers engaged and invested in the story (Hodges, 2017). Concentrate on developing a captivating story arc with a distinct beginning, middle, and finish. Develop a series of events and conflicts that challenge your characters and drive the story forward. Ensure that each scene and chapter serves a purpose and contributes to the plot progression.

Literary devices add richness and depth to your writing. Foreshadowing, for example, hints at future events and creates anticipation (Hodges, 2017). Symbolism can convey deeper meanings and themes using objects, actions, or settings to represent abstract ideas. By skillfully incorporating these devices, you can enhance the complexity and impact of your storytelling. Instead of simply telling readers what is happening, aim to show them through vivid descriptions, actions, and dialogue. Use sensory details, strong verbs, and figurative language to create a visual and immersive experience. Show characters' emotions through their behavior and interactions, allowing readers to infer their feelings rather than explicitly stating them. Varying sentence structure helps maintain reader interest and adds rhythm to your writing. Experiment with sentence length and structure to create a flow that matches the mood and pace of your story.

Short, punchy sentences can convey tension or urgency, while longer, more descriptive sentences can set a slower pace or emphasize essential details.

Reading widely exposes you to different writing styles, genres, and techniques. Pay attention to how successful authors handle character development, plot progression, and the use of literary devices. Analyze their writing to understand how they create impact and engage readers. Incorporate the lessons learned into your writing, adapting them to your unique voice and style. Writing is a process, and revision is essential for improving your style. Take time to review and edit your work with a critical eye. Look for areas where you can tighten sentences, clarify ideas, or enhance descriptions. Cut unnecessary words and phrases to improve clarity and conciseness. Seek feedback from others, such as beta readers or writing groups, to gain different perspectives on your writing (Hodges, 2017). Remember, as you embark on your writing adventure, developing your unique style is a gradual process that requires dedication and practice. Explore the vast landscape of literary devices, experimenting with their various shades and hues. With time, your style will bloom and evolve, reflecting your distinctive voice and captivating readers with the symphony of devices.

Key Takeaways

Crafting compelling and authentic dialogue requires mirroring natural speech patterns while maintaining conciseness and purpose. Pay meticulous attention to your characters' rhythm, tone, and vocabulary, allowing their unique personalities and backgrounds to shine through their spoken words. Instead of explicitly stating emotions, conflicts, and relationships, leverage dialogue as a tool to show them, adding depth and authenticity to character interactions. Ensure that each conversation serves a purpose in advancing the plot, whether it's revealing crucial information, introducing conflicts or obstacles, or contributing to character development.

Embrace the power of subtext in your dialogue, where characters imply or hint at underlying meanings and intentions. This subtle layer of complexity and intrigue encourages readers to delve deeper, interpreting the unsaid and engaging with the story more profoundly. To maintain a dynamic balance between dialogue and description, seamlessly weave conversations into your narrative, breaking up long passages and infusing the story with variety. By incorporating dialogue within your descriptions, you can offer character interactions and their reactions to the surrounding environment, further enhancing their depth and relatability.

When it comes to descriptions, remember to infuse them with purpose. Each description should serve a specific function within the story, whether setting the mood, enhancing characterization, advancing the plot, or creating symbolism. Avoid excessive or irrelevant details that don't contribute to the overall narrative. Engage your readers' senses by incorporating sensory details. Visual descriptions can be achieved through descriptive adjectives, painting a vivid picture of the setting and characters. Auditory details can be captured by employing onomatopoeia, descriptive verbs, and comparisons. Describing scents can evoke powerful emotions and transport readers into the story's world. At the same time, taste sensations can deepen their connection to the narrative. Additionally, tactile descriptions that utilize adjectives and similes can engage readers physically, immersing them further in the story's events.

Incorporating literary devices such as metaphors, similes, and other figures of speech can elevate your descriptions, creating vivid and evocative imagery. Choose sensory details selectively, focusing on those most relevant to the scene, character, or atmosphere. Each sensory detail should serve a purpose, contributing to the overall narrative and enhancing the reader's experience. Ultimately, developing your writing style takes time and practice. By embracing character development, constructing a robust plot, utilizing literary devices, showing rather than telling, varying sentence structures, reading widely, and revising and editing your work, you can create a vivid and immersive reading experience for your audience.

6

CREATING CONFLICT AND PLOT DEVELOPMENT

Conflict is the driving force behind compelling storytelling, and its effective implementation is essential for creating engaging plots that captivate readers. In this chapter, we will explore the significance of conflict in plot development and its pivotal role in shaping narratives. Conflict introduces tension, challenges, and obstacles that propel characters forward and test their resilience, ultimately driving the story's momentum. By delving into different types of conflict, from internal struggles to external clashes, we will uncover how they contribute to character growth, plot progression, and reader engagement.

Furthermore, we will examine the relationship between conflict and character development, as conflicts force characters to confront their fears, face moral dilemmas, and undergo transformative journeys. Understanding the intricacies of conflict and its impact on plot development empowers writers to craft compelling stories that resonate with readers on emotional and intellectual levels. Throughout this chapter, we will provide practical tips, examples, and exercises to help you master the art of conflict and utilize it as a potent tool for driving your narratives forward. I implore you to delve into the heart of conflict and unlock the full potential of your storytelling abilities.

Creating Tension and Conflict in Your Story

In storytelling, conflict is vital in driving the narrative forward and creating tension and excitement for the readers or viewers. Selecting conflicts with significant meaning and relevance is crucial when crafting conflicts for your characters. These conflicts should resonate with their values, goals, and motivations, thereby making them more engaging and relatable to the audience. Mastering the art of creating tension in storytelling is essential for crafting a captivating narrative that keeps readers hooked. Crafting a gripping and immersive read involves several vital elements.

Crucial conflict: Select conflicts that genuinely matter to your characters. Identify their first goals, and introduce tension or friction that stands in their way. Whether it's a disagreement with parents or a more significant fate-of-the-universe conflict, make sure it relates to what your characters value most.

Engaging characters: Make your readers care about your characters by making them exciting and relatable. Create engaging dynamics through opposing goals, views, and personalities. This can lead to intriguing and tense character interactions, allowing readers to connect with different characters in the story.

Raise The Stakes

Build narrative suspense and tension by having your protagonist encounter obstacles and experience failures.

Even if they succeed initially, hint at adverse consequences in the background.

Follow the rule of threes, with two unsuccessful attempts before the third successful one, to structure rising conflict and keep the story engaging.

Ebb and flow of tension: Pace your story by balancing moments of tension with quieter periods. Constant high tension can exhaust readers, so incorporate smaller moments of tension and ease throughout the narrative. Gradually intensify the tension leading to the climax, but provide pauses along the way.

Internal and external conflict: Create tension from external forces and internal struggles. External conflicts can involve physical confrontations or survival challenges. In contrast, internal conflicts reflect inner struggles, difficult choices, flaws, vulnerabilities, and weaknesses. The two types of tension can intertwine and reinforce each other.

Secondary sources of tension: Just like in real life, characters can face multiple tensions and challenges simultaneously. Consider the various aspects of your characters' lives. And introduce secondary sources of tension that add complexity to their journeys. Juggling different conflicts can make the story more dynamic and realistic.

Shorter time frame: If suitable for your story, condense the narrative into a shorter time frame. Set a sense of urgency, and create a fast-paced environment requiring immediate resolution. This approach, often seen in TV series or thriller novels, can heighten tension and keep readers engaged.

By incorporating these elements into your storytelling, you can create a gripping narrative that captivates readers from beginning to end (Writer's Relief, 2022). Revise, edit, and seek feedback to polish your work and ensure a compelling reading experience. Remember, the conflicts you create should serve a purpose in your story and contribute to the overall narrative arc. By selecting conflicts that genuinely matter to your characters and relating them to their deepest values, you can engage your audience, evoke empathy, and create a more immersive storytelling experience.

Developing a Strong Plot

Developing a solid plot is essential for creating a compelling and engaging novel. A well-crafted plot keeps readers hooked, propels the story forward, and provides a structure for the narrative. It involves several key steps. Firstly, it's essential to understand the distinction between plot-driven and character-driven narratives. Plot-driven narratives focus on the sequence of events and twists, captivating the audience with excitement and engagement. On the other hand, character-driven narratives delve into the inner lives of protagonists and their psychological development, adding depth and complexity to the story.

A well-rounded story requires both well-drawn characters and a solidly constructed plot. To build a strong plot, consider the six main elements: exposition, conflict or inciting incident, rising action, climax, falling action, and resolution. These elements provide a framework for your narrative, guiding the progression of events and creating a satisfying story arc. To generate ideas for your plot, you can start by brainstorming a list of events that could ignite the story. Drawing inspiration from personal experiences, observations, and external sources can help fuel your creativity. Once you have a pool of ideas, it's crucial to create a premise that expresses the proposed plot in simple terms, capturing the essence of the story and its central conflict.

Developing your characters is equally important. You can start by writing brief profiles and backstories for each significant character, exploring their motivations, strengths, weaknesses, and personal histories. These details will contribute to their development and influence their actions within the plot. Choosing settings for your story can enhance its richness and believability. Creating visual collages or mood boards can inspire vivid descriptions and provide a reference point for your writing. Introducing the central conflict or problem early on in your narrative is critical to creating tension and anchoring the plot. This conflict should pulsate with significance, its stakes reaching towering heights that seize the characters' essence, igniting their actions with an unquenchable infernal driving force—propelling the story along its captivating trajectory.

Mapping out a logical cause-and-effect path from the conflict to the climax and resolution is essential. Storyboarding through sketches or outlining can help visualize the plot arc and ensure a cohesive and satisfying narrative flow. To craft a strong plot, there are some general guidelines to keep in mind:

- Begin with a solid hook to immediately capture the readers' attention.
- Understand the genre you're writing in and tailor your plot accordingly.
- Create memorable characters that readers can connect with and root for.

- Build conflict throughout the story, increasing the stakes and creating obstacles for your characters to overcome.
- Utilize the three-act structure to provide balanced pacing and progression.
- Introduce twists and turns to keep the story engaging and unpredictable.
- Keep the plot relatively simple, avoiding unnecessary complications.
- Use foreshadowing to hint at future events and create anticipation.
- Ensure a clear resolution that ties up loose ends and provides a satisfying conclusion.
- Finally, write passionately and enthusiastically, infusing your narrative with emotion and authenticity (How To Write a Great Plot, 2023).

In the hands of a skillful storyteller, these guiding principles transform into a portal that transports readers to captivating realms. They become the map leading them through treacherous jungles of suspense, across vast oceans of emotion, and up mountain peaks of exhilaration. With each page turn, your plot becomes an enchanting journey where readers are swept away on the wings of imagination, utterly captivated by the world you've meticulously crafted.

Understanding Story Structure

Writing a compelling story can be an arduous task, especially for newcomers. The abundance of conflicting advice online can easily overwhelm you and make you contemplate giving up before even starting. However, it's important to remember that you possess more knowledge and understanding than you realize. Stories are integral to our lives, permeating various mediums such as music, television, video games, books, and movies. Every story follows a familiar pattern regardless of its genre or plot. (Jenkins, 2022).

This storytelling template, popularized by Joseph Campbell's The Hero with a Thousand Faces, outlines 17 stages that can be found in every story ever told. In 1985, screenwriter Christopher Vogler condensed these 17 stages into 12 in his memo for Disney titled The Practical Guide to Joseph Campbell's The Hero with a Thousand Faces. This modified Hero's Journey template has influenced storytellers worldwide, including renowned creators like George Lucas (Jenkins, 2022). It is essential to comprehend the three main stages of The Hero's Journey.

1. **The Departure:** The hero is compelled to leave their ordinary world. They may have doubts or concerns, and this is where a mentor can provide encouragement and guidance. For instance, in The Hunger Games (Collins, 2008), the protagonist, Katniss Everdeen, is a devoted sister, daughter, and friend. As the looming Hunger Games threaten her and her friends, she fears the possibility of being chosen.
2. **Initiation:** The hero enters a new world and faces various obstacles. They may face these challenges alone or with companions. Here, they must utilize the skills and tools acquired from their ordinary life to overcome each obstacle and eventually return to their initial world with a reward. In The Hunger Games, Katniss offers to stand in for her sister as a tribute. Alongside Peeta, the baker's son, she is whisked away for training and the competition itself.

3. **Return:** The hero returns to their everyday life, which now appears different due to their transformation. They bring back the rewards they have obtained and use them for the greater good. In The Hunger Games, Katniss and Peeta emerge as victors, having decided to defy the Capitol's rules. They survive and become celebrities, forever changed by their experiences.

Consider the twelve steps within the phases mentioned to effectively utilize The Hero's Journey in your own story (Jenkins, 2022).

Departure

1. **Ordinary world:** Introduce your hero in their everyday environment, showing their human side and what drives them.
2. **The call to adventure:** Present a problem, challenge, or adventure that will forever change the hero's world.
3. **Refusal of the call:** Sometimes, the hero hesitates when faced with adversity, but they must overcome their fears and proceed.

4. **Meeting with the mentor:** Introduce a mentor figure who provides guidance, wisdom, or necessary tools for the protagonist's journey.
5. **Crossing the first threshold:** The hero must gather courage and step into the new world, solidifying the underlying theme and stakes of the story.

Initiation

1. **Tests, allies, and enemies:** The hero encounters challenges, forms alliances, and faces chaos while being tested and challenged.
2. **Approach to the inmost cave:** The hero faces hidden dangers and their greatest fears, requiring them to dig deep and find courage.
3. **The Ordeal:** The hero experiences their darkest moment and greatest challenge, undergoing significant transformation.
4. **Reward (seizing the sword):** The hero emerges victorious, having defeated enemies and undergone an inward and outward change.

Return

1. **The road back:** The hero begins their return to the ordinary world but realizes the battle is not yet over, facing consequences for their actions.
2. **The resurrection:** The hero confronts their final and most threatening challenge, possibly facing death again.
3. **Return with the elixir:** The hero triumphantly crosses back into their ordinary life, forever changed by the adventure, bringing rewards and impacting their life in unforeseen ways.

The Hero's Journey can be observed in numerous well-known stories, such as *Sleeping Beauty, Star Wars, Lord of the Rings, The Hobbit, Indiana Jones, Sherlock Holmes, Jane Eyre, Pilgrim's Progress, The Wizard of Oz, and Toy Story.*

Using Plot Devices to Enhance Your Story

Plot devices are powerful tools that writers use to craft compelling narratives. They add depth, intrigue, and suspense to the story, keeping readers engaged and invested. There are several common plot devices found in various forms of fiction.

One commonly used plot device is the "red herring." This involves introducing a seemingly important element or clue that later turns out to be a mere distraction, diverting attention from the true significance of the story.

Another effective plot device is the "plot voucher" or "Chekov's Gun" (Masterclass, 2021e) around introducing a character, object, or detail early in the story that holds significance or plays a crucial role later on. This principle ensures that every element introduced in the narrative serves a purpose.

The "MacGuffin" is a plot device often employed in adventure or mystery stories. It revolves around an object or goal that the characters pursue relentlessly, driving the plot forward (MasterClass, 2021e). While the MacGuffin may hold little intrinsic value, its pursuit creates conflict and propels the story.

Love triangles are a common plot device in romantic or dramatic narratives. They involve three characters, two in love with the third. This dynamic creates tension, jealousy, and emotional conflicts that impact relationships and character development.

A quest is a plot device often used in fantasy or adventure stories. Characters embark on a journey or mission driven by a central goal. The quest structure allows exploring diverse settings, encountering new characters, and developing multiple subplots.

Cliffhangers are powerful plot devices that leave readers on the edge of their seats. They occur when a section of the story ends abruptly without providing a resolution. This creates suspense and anticipation, compelling readers to continue reading to discover what happens next.

The "deus ex machina" plot device introduces an unexpected and often contrived solution to resolve conflicts within the story (MasterClass, 2021e). While it can provide a quick resolution, it is often seen as a narrative shortcut that may undermine the sense of realism or earned resolutions.

To effectively use plot devices in your writing, consider the following tips:

- Enhance your core story. Plot devices should complement and enhance the main narrative rather than be used as mere distractions or shortcuts.

- Focus on solid storytelling, well-developed characters, and world-building as the foundation of your story.
- Maintain organic integration. Plot devices should seamlessly integrate into the narrative, maintaining the reader's suspension of disbelief.
- Avoid forced or clunky implementations that distract from the story itself.

Differentiate between plot devices and literary devices. While both can enhance your writing, literary devices primarily focus on language and style. In contrast, plot devices drive the story forward. Understand the distinction and use them appropriately. By understanding and effectively utilizing these plot devices, you can create engaging and impactful narratives that captivate your readers, leaving them eager to unravel the intricacies of your story.

Key Takeaways

When crafting your story, choose conflicts that resonate with your characters' desires, fears, and values, engaging readers. Give characters opposing goals and distinct personalities to create natural conflict. Introduce obstacles and failures for the protagonist, maintaining reader interest. Balance tension with quieter moments for pacing. Use external and internal conflicts to add depth. Add complexity with subplots, secondary characters, or additional challenges. Condense the timeline for urgency. Understand the difference between plot-driven and character-driven narratives. Follow storytelling elements: exposition, conflict, rising action, climax, falling action, and resolution. Develop well-rounded characters with motivations and backstories. Choose settings that enhance the story.

Introduce a significant conflict early on to engage readers. Create a logical cause-and-effect path. Utilize hooks and foreshadowing. Familiarize yourself with The Hero's Journey and employ its stages and steps. Use plot devices like red herrings, Chekov's Gun, MacGuffins, love triangles, quests, and cliffhangers. Differentiate between plot devices and literary devices, such as symbolism, metaphors, and irony. Plot devices drive the narrative forward, while literary devices add depth and layers of meaning to the story. Both can be utilized effectively to create an engaging and impactful narrative. By integrating these narrative gems seamlessly into their storytelling alchemy, writers forge a bond with their readers, holding them captive within the world they have created. These carefully placed plot points become the riddles and clues readers eagerly unravel, fostering an immersive and satisfying literary experience.

7

MANAGING PACING AND TENSION

Pacing and tension play integral roles in captivating readers and keeping them engrossed in the narrative. The artful manipulation of pacing and tension is akin to orchestrating a symphony, with each beat and crescendo carefully crafted to evoke emotions and propel the story forward. A well-paced novel strikes a delicate balance, allowing readers to breathe and savor quieter moments while ratcheting up the tension during pivotal scenes. The interplay between pacing and tension creates a dynamic rhythm that keeps readers on the edge of their seats, eagerly turning pages to uncover what lies ahead. Understanding the mechanics of pacing and tension empowers writers to wield these tools effectively, heightening the reader's experience and ensuring that the story unfolds in a captivating and satisfying manner.

In this chapter, we probe into the intricacies of pacing and tension, exploring how they work in tandem to drive the narrative, create suspense, and maintain reader engagement. We will examine techniques and strategies to masterfully manipulate the pace of your story, balancing moments of reflection and action to create a compelling rhythm. Additionally, we will explore the various sources of tension, from external conflicts to internal struggles, and discover how to amplify and release tension to maintain a gripping narrative arc. By the end of this chapter, you will possess a deeper understanding of the vital role that pacing and tension play in crafting a mesmerizing novel, equipping you with the tools to captivate readers and keep them enthralled from beginning to end.

Maintaining the Pacing of Your Story

Break down the structure of your story and analyze the main events and plot points. It's essential to identify where the pacing needs adjustments. By visually mapping out the flow of your story, you can determine the areas that require increased or decreased pace. This breakdown will help you clearly understand the narrative's rhythm and allow you to make necessary modifications. You may manage the tempo by changing the spacing between phrases, paragraphs, and chapters (Bradshaw, 2020). Short and choppy sentences and paragraphs create a fast-paced feel, propelling the story forward with quick momentum. On the other hand, longer sentences and paragraphs slow things down, offering a more leisurely pace that allows for deeper exploration and reflection.

Consider employing heightened detail to slow down the pacing for specific moments. By providing vivid descriptions and focusing on sensory experiences, you intensify the reader's immersion and emphasize the importance of particular scenes or events. This technique acts like a slow-motion shot in a movie, drawing attention and adding depth to crucial moments in your story. Incorporating introspection and internal monologue is another effective way to slow down the pace and develop your characters. Delving into their thoughts, emotions, and motivations gives readers a deeper understanding and connection to the characters. This introspective approach adds layers to their development and allows a more profound exploration of their inner worlds.

During the editing process, evaluate the necessity of each element in your story. Consider whether they contribute to the plot, character development, or reader experience. Eliminate elements that don't serve a purpose, as they can unnecessarily slow the pacing (Bradshaw, 2020). Streamlining your narrative will ensure that every scene and detail actively contributes to the story's progression. Seeking feedback from beta readers or critique partners is invaluable when assessing the pacing of your story. Sharing your work with others and asking for their insights can illuminate areas where the pacing may lag or feel rushed. Their perspective as readers will help you identify and address any pacing issues you might have overlooked.

Remembering good pacing doesn't always mean a consistently fast-paced narrative is essential. Pacing is about finding the right balance between fast and slow sections. While fast-paced scenes create excitement and tension, slower-paced sections are necessary for character development, providing contrast and allowing readers to process information. In understanding this balance, you can create a dynamic and engaging story that captivates readers from start to finish. When you implement these tips, you can achieve a well-paced story that keeps readers engaged and maintains a balanced rhythm.

Building Tension and Suspense

Build well-rounded and relatable characters that readers can become attached to. Give them conflicting goals and motivations, naturally creating tension as they strive to achieve their objectives. Determine what your characters stand to gain or lose based on the outcome of their actions. Increase the stakes by raising the potential rewards for success or the consequences of failure (Jordan, 2021). This raises the tension and makes the story more engaging. Introduce obstacles and challenges for your characters to overcome. Conflict drives the story forward and allows your characters to grow and learn. If the story feels as if it's lacking in tension, consider adding new problems or reviving old ones to keep the suspense building and readers on the edge of their seats.

Give your characters a limited amount of time to achieve their goals. A deadline adds urgency and desperation to their actions, increasing tension and captivating the story. Alongside the main plotline, develop smaller subplots and increase tension and suspense. Well-crafted subplots can provide additional momentum to the story and make it feel more dynamic. However, be mindful not to overwhelm the story with too many subplots, which may lead to plot holes. Control the pacing of your story to build tension effectively. You could speed up key scenes to engage readers and make them feel like the story is moving faster. Alternatively, use shorter sentences, back-to-back action, and less description during intense moments to create a sense of urgency.

Withhold crucial information from your characters and readers until an opportune moment in the story. This revelation should change the characters' plans or introduce a new deadline, adding urgency and heightening the suspense. Surprise your readers and characters with unexpected events or developments. Plot twists require the characters to adapt quickly, creating tension and suspense. Foreshadow subtly throughout the story, but make sure the twists are surprising. Some writers temporarily slow down the pacing in certain moments to give readers a break from intense tension. These moments of rest and relief make the tension peaks feel even more dramatic and surprising. End chapters or sections with cliffhangers that pose compelling questions or create a sense of impending danger (Jordan, 2021).

This technique entices readers to continue reading and builds suspense. However, use cliffhangers sparingly to maintain their impact.

Remember to maintain control over your tension and suspense. Ensure that any devices or twists you incorporate logically fit within the story's narrative. Well-plotted elements will have a more substantial impact on readers and create a more satisfying reading experience.

Using Cliffhangers and Other Techniques

A cliffhanger is a literary device that creates suspense and keeps readers engaged by ending a scene, chapter, or book without resolving the questions or conflicts raised. It leaves the audience hanging, eagerly wanting to know what happens next. The term originated from a Thomas Hardy serial where a character was left hanging off a cliff. Cliffhangers have a long history and were popularized in works like One Thousand and One Nights (1775) and Victorian serial novels by authors like Charles Dickens (Patterson, 2018). They are also commonly used in television series, with the famous example of "Who Shot JR?" in Dallas (Patterson, 2018). In modern writing, cliffhangers are even more prevalent, as they help maintain suspense and capture readers' attention. They serve as practical pacing tools, enticing readers to turn the page and continue reading. James Patterson, for example, often uses short chapters that end with unresolved situations.

Here are 10 types of cliffhangers that effectively engage readers:

- An unanswered question: Pose a thought-provoking question or leave the initial question unanswered to create curiosity.
- A loss: Introduce a physical or emotional loss the protagonist believes they can't live without.
- Dangle a carrot: Show the character something they desperately desire but is just out of reach.
- A glimmer of hope: Hint at an upcoming event or development that offers excitement or change.
- A physical threat: End with the character or someone they care about in immediate danger, compelling readers to continue.
- A sense of foreboding: Use foreshadowing, body language, signs, and symbols to convey a risky situation.

- A ticking clock: Set a deadline that must be reached to instill a feeling of urgency.
- An accident: Introduce an unexpected event, such as a physical accident or a slip of the tongue, which disrupts the situation.
- Unexpected news: Reveal important or devastating information or introduce an unexpected character.
- An unmade decision: Leave a character with a crucial decision that needs to be made.

By skillfully deploying cliffhangers, writers wield the power to ensnare readers, captivating their attention and preserving their curiosity as the story unfolds (Patterson, 2018). These suspenseful strategic pauses leave readers yearning to discover what develops with the next page turn.

Avoiding Common Pacing Problems

When crafting your story, avoiding too much information (TMI) in the plot is essential (Valentine, 2019). Instead, provide only the necessary information to the reader, measuring the details carefully, like ingredients in a recipe. This ensures the story flows smoothly without overwhelming the reader with unnecessary or excessive information. Avoid information dumps where vital background information is provided all at once. Instead, distribute these details gradually throughout the story, allowing them to unfold naturally. This keeps the reader engaged and curious, revealing essential elements as treats.

While journalism often presents information concisely and upfront, fiction should unfold gradually. Introduce essential elements gradually, building suspense and intrigue for the reader. This gradual revelation keeps the story captivating and immerses readers in the narrative. To keep the story moving, only mundane actions and routines if they serve a purpose in the plot. Summarize everyday activities that don't contribute significantly to the story, focusing on the events and actions that propel the plot forward.

Exercise restraint when describing characters. Beware of excess character description and focus on key characteristics that reveal their personality or differentiate them from others. You may give readers valuable insights into the characters while letting them create their mental images by employing descriptive information sparingly and intentionally. When it comes to setting descriptions, balance providing enough information to establish the setting and avoiding excessive detail (Valentine, 2019). Specificity is important, but too much detail can bog down the story's pacing. Provide an outline for readers' imaginations to fill in, allowing them to visualize the setting without overwhelming them with unnecessary specifics.

Ensure that dialogue serves a purpose in the story. Avoid aimless or mundane conversations that do not contribute to character development or plot progression. Instead, ensure that dialogue reveals something significant about the plot or characters, advancing the story or providing necessary information. Establish the setting to give readers a sense of place. Avoid floating characters by providing context and grounding the story in a specific location (Valentine, 2019). This helps readers visualize the story's environment and enhances their reading experience.

When describing settings, suggest rather than sculpt in stone. Give readers enough information to locate the scene without overwhelming them with unnecessary specifics. This allows readers to engage their imagination and actively participate in the story. Simplify and streamline the narrative by balancing action and relevant details. Stay aware of overly descriptive passages that slow down the pacing. Focus on conveying the essential elements while keeping the story dynamic and engaging. Applying these suggestions can help your novel's pacing and keep readers interested throughout the narrative.

Key Takeaways

Breaking down its structure and carefully adjusting the pacing is essential when crafting your story. One effective technique is to vary the length of sentences, paragraphs, and even chapters, allowing for precise control over the rhythm and tempo of your narrative. To slow down the pace and immerse readers in the moment, employ heightened detail and introspection, painting a vivid picture that captivates their senses. Streamlining the narrative requires evaluating the necessity of each element, ensuring that every component contributes to the whole plot and characterization.

To address pacing issues, seek feedback from trusted sources, welcoming insights that can help fine-tune the pacing to maximize reader engagement. Developing conflicted characters with high stakes adds depth and intensity to your story, making readers emotionally invested in their journeys. Introduce obstacles and set tight deadlines, creating a sense of urgency that propels the plot forward. Alongside the main storyline, increase tension in subplots, intertwining them with the central narrative to maintain a gripping sense of intrigue. Control the pacing by incorporating shorter sentences and injecting action-packed moments that keep readers on the edge of their seats. Employ big reveals and plot twists, expertly crafted to surprise and captivate your audience, leaving them hungry for more.

While cliffhangers can be a powerful tool, use them sparingly to provide moments of relief and suspense, leaving questions unanswered and enticing readers to eagerly anticipate the next installment. There are various cliffhangers at your disposal, such as posing unanswered questions, inflicting losses upon characters, offering glimpses of hope amidst adversity, presenting physical threats, utilizing foreshadowing, and introducing ticking clocks, accidents, unexpected news, and unresolved decisions. Implement these cliffhangers strategically at pivotal moments, leaving readers yearning for resolution and eager to continue the narrative.

It is crucial to provide the necessary information to avoid overwhelming readers with excessive exposition. Avoid information dumps by gradually unfolding the story and revealing key details at the right moments to maintain a sense of mystery and intrigue. Skip mundane actions and focus on plot-propelling events that drive the story forward, engaging readers through compelling twists and turns. Restrain character and setting descriptions to the essentials, allowing readers to fill in the details with their imaginations. Ensure that dialogue serves a purpose, conveying important information, revealing character traits, or advancing the plot. Establishing the setting effectively and simplifying the narrative allows readers to immerse themselves in your created world without unnecessary distractions. By carefully considering each of these elements and employing them with skill and finesse, you can masterfully control the pacing of your story, ensuring a captivating and satisfying reading experience for your audience.

8

RAPID REVISING AND EDITING

Iterative and dynamic writing includes putting words on paper and revising and polishing them. In this chapter, we delve into the essential skills of revising and editing, which are crucial for transforming a rough draft into a refined masterpiece. Whether you're a student working on an essay, a professional crafting a report, or a novelist developing a novel, mastering these techniques will significantly enhance your written work's clarity, coherence, and effectiveness.

To begin, we explore strategies for revising quickly. We understand that time is often a precious commodity, and revising an entire piece of writing can seem daunting. However, you can streamline the revision process without sacrificing quality by employing efficient techniques and focusing on critical areas. We'll discuss methods such as identifying weak spots, clarifying arguments, and improving the flow of your writing to help you make significant revisions in a timely manner.

Next, we highlight common mistakes to look for during the revision process. No matter how careful or experienced a writer you are, errors can slip through the cracks. By familiarizing yourself with the most frequent stumbling blocks, such as grammatical errors, punctuation mistakes, awkward sentence structures, or inconsistencies in style and tone, you can develop a keen eye for catching and rectifying them. This chapter will provide practical tips on identifying and rectifying these common pitfalls.

Additionally, we address the crucial topic of when to ask for feedback. Seeking input from others can be invaluable in improving your work. We discuss the importance of choosing the right individuals to provide feedback and how to effectively communicate your expectations and concerns. Whether it's a peer, mentor, or professional editor, we offer guidance on utilizing feedback to enhance your writing and take it to the next level.

Finally, we delve into the art of editing your work. While revision focuses on the larger picture and content, editing zeroes in on the smaller elements can significantly improve the caliber of your work. From ensuring proper grammar and punctuation to refining word choice, sentence structure, and paragraph transitions, we provide practical tips and techniques to help you polish your writing until it shines.

With the strategies, insights, and tools presented in this chapter, you will gain the confidence and skills to tackle the revising and editing process with finesse. Revising quickly, identifying common mistakes, seeking valuable feedback, and mastering the art of editing, will transform your writing into a compelling and impactful piece that enthralls book lovers.

Strategies for Revising Quickly

Proofreading serves as the final step in the writing process, aimed at identifying and rectifying grammar, punctuation, spelling, and formatting errors. Its purpose is to ensure the written work is polished and devoid of slipups that could hinder comprehension or undermine the writer's reliability. Implementing effective proofreading techniques can significantly enhance the quality of your writing. To begin, taking a break before starting the proofreading process is recommended. Similar to the revision stage, stepping away from the text for a while allows the writer to approach it with fresh eyes. This new perspective often identifies errors and inconsistencies that may have been overlooked during the initial writing phase (Research Guides, 2021).

When proofreading, it is crucial to read the text slowly and attentively. Each word, sentence, and punctuation mark should be carefully scrutinized. Reading quickly increases the chances of overlooking blunders, so a deliberate and focused reading pace is advised. Additionally, employing the technique of reading the text backward can be beneficial. Starting from the last sentence and working one's way up to the beginning helps isolate individual words and prevents the brain from automatically correcting errors. While grammar and spell-check tools can be helpful, they should not be relied upon exclusively. These tools can assist in catching common mistakes, but they may also miss specific errors or suggest incorrect corrections. Therefore, it is essential to proofread the writing multiple times, with each pass concentrating on different aspects, such as grammar, punctuation, and spelling (Research Guides, 2021). This iterative approach to proofreading helps maintain concentration and allows for detecting a broader range of errors.

Seeking a second opinion is another valuable strategy in the proofreading process. Asking someone else to review the writing can provide fresh insights and perspectives. Others often notice errors or inconsistencies the writer might have missed due to their familiarity with the text. The input of a second proofreader can significantly enhance the overall quality of the work. In addition to checking for grammatical and spelling errors, attention should be given to formatting. Ensuring that the writing adheres to consistent font usage, spacing, margins, and any other formatting requirements dictated by the specific style guidelines. Consistency in formatting enhances the professional appearance of the work and contributes to its readability.

A meticulous and detail-oriented approach is essential in proofreading. It is crucial to look for common errors such as missing or extra words, incorrect punctuation, subject-verb agreement, and verb tense consistency. Attention to detail is vital in identifying these subtle mistakes that can significantly impact the clarity and coherence of your writing. Incorporating these revision, editing, and proofreading tips into the writing process can greatly enhance your work's clarity, organization, and effectiveness (Research Guides, 2021). It's important to remember that writing is a craft that requires practice and attention to detail. Regularly applying these proofreading techniques will enhance the quality of the current work and contribute to developing strong writing skills in the long run.

When to Request Feedback

The decision of when to ask for feedback on your new story can vary depending on personal preference and the specific needs of your writing process. Receiving feedback at different stages of the writing process can greatly benefit writers, and it starts with the plot outline. Some writers find seeking feedback on their plot outline valuable before embarking on the first draft. By doing so, they can ensure that the story structure and major plot points are solid, saving them time and effort in writing an entire manuscript that might require significant revisions later. Once the first draft is completed, seeking feedback becomes even more important. At this stage, writers may seek input on the story's effectiveness. They are interested in understanding how well the plot unfolds, the characters' development, the narrative's pacing, and any significant issues that may arise with the plot (When to Ask for Feedback, 2018). This feedback provides valuable insights into the strengths and weaknesses of the story, allowing writers to make informed decisions during the revision process.

After incorporating revisions and significant changes, seeking feedback becomes crucial during the second draft. This time, the focus can shift toward more specific elements of the writing. Writers may seek feedback on the quality of dialogue, the style of prose, the consistency of the narrative, and any lingering issues with plot or character development. This feedback helps writers refine their writing, ensures the story flows smoothly, and engages readers effectively. As the story nears completion and substantial revisions have been made, writers may consider sharing their work with a select group of trusted readers. These readers can provide feedback from the perspective of a potential audience, giving insights into the reading experience. Their feedback can help writers gauge the impact and effectiveness of the story, identify strengths and weaknesses, and make final adjustments before sharing their work more widely (When to Ask for Feedback, 2018).

The type of feedback sought at each stage of the writing process depends on the writer's specific goals and needs. However, it is essential to consider aspects such as the strength of the story structure, character arcs, major plot points, overall impressions, character development, pacing, dialogue, prose style, consistency, and appeal to a potential audience. Incorporating feedback at different stages of the writing process allows writers to craft a more potent and engaging final piece of work.

Tips for Editing Your Work

Reviewing a book may be difficult, especially when revising your writing. However, there are several steps you can follow to make the process less painful and more effective.

Before diving into the editing process, take some time to clarify your book's main point or message. Write multiple synopses from different perspectives to clearly understand what's important to convey. Instead of making immediate edits, read through your book without making any changes

(Research Guides, 2021). Take notes on the edits you want to make and gather feedback from beta readers or writing partners. This allows you to gather insights and evaluate the overall structure before making specific edits. Establish goals for the quality and timeline of your editing process. Focus on making your writing clean, concise, and easily understood. Determine the desired pace of editing, such as editing a certain number of chapters per week. Here are some other tips:

- Breaking your book into manageable sections can make editing more organized and less overwhelming. Divide the book into sections based on the three-act structure or teaching sections for nonfiction (Research Guides, 2021).
- Characters play a significant role in engaging readers. Evaluate each character's purpose, ensuring they are attractive, serve a clear role, and have completed arcs.
- Assess each chapter for its purpose in advancing the plot or teaching points. Remove or condense chapters that don't contribute to the general storyline or message.

- Ensure each chapter can stand alone and contribute to the book's flow. Maintain a suitable pace throughout the book by managing the overall pacing and pacing within chapters.
- Vary paragraph length and structure to control the pacing, using shorter paragraphs and more dialogue for faster-paced sections and longer, descriptive paragraphs for slower-paced sections (Research Guides, 2021).
- Perform a line-by-line edit to eliminate typos and grammatical mistakes and to improve readability. Ask yourself questions about each sentence and paragraph to ensure clarity and coherence.
- Consider rearranging sentences for better flow and readability. While editing, it's essential to avoid common mistakes, such as overcomplicating the writing, using redundancies, and neglecting simplicity and clarity.

Remember, editing is a detailed process, and seeking professional help from a book editor can greatly enhance the final product.

Key Takeaways

Take breaks, read slowly and attentively, read the text backward, use grammar and spell-check tools as a supplement, proofread multiple times, seek a second opinion, pay attention to formatting, and be meticulous in identifying common errors such as grammar, punctuation, spelling, and formatting errors. Also, inconsistencies in style, tense, and subject-verb agreement are some of the usual suspects to look out for while reviewing a book. Seek feedback on the plot outline before starting the first draft. Get feedback on the first draft for overall story effectiveness, character development, pacing, and major plot issues. Seek feedback on the second draft for specific elements like dialogue, prose style, consistency, and remaining plot or character issues. Share the near-completed story with trusted readers for insights into the overall reading experience and final adjustments. Define your book's main point or message, do a read through without editing, set editing goals, break the book into sections, focus on characters or people, edit chapters for purpose and contribution, consider pacing, and perform a line-by-line edit for clarity and readability.

9

PURSUING WRITING AS A CAREER

In the literary world, where the possibilities are as vast and diverse as the imagination itself, if you have a burning desire to become a writer and unleash your creativity upon the world, you have embarked on an exhilarating journey filled with exploration, growth, and endless opportunities.

One of your first steps is discovering your genre, the literary landscape where your unique voice can thrive. Whether you have a natural inclination toward a specific genre or are eager to explore various genres until you find your niche, this process of self-discovery is essential. Experiment with different styles, dive into short stories or memoirs, or venture into fiction, mystery, romance, or science fiction. An exciting life can provide a wealth of anecdotes and experiences that make for compelling storytelling (Bleiweiss, 2023).

However, discovering your genre is just the beginning. To truly excel as a writer, you must master the craft. Invest in your writing skills by taking classes, studying grammar, and immersing yourself in books on the art of writing. Continuous learning and improvement will enhance your abilities and increase your chances of success. Remember, writing is a creative outlet and a discipline that requires dedication and perseverance.

Consistency is critical to sharpening your sword and finding your voice. Write consistently and extensively, embracing the journey of creation and revision. Every piece of writing you produce is an opportunity for growth, and you never know which work will be your best or most commercially viable until you've written multiple pieces. Consider submitting your short stories or articles to magazines for exposure and valuable feedback.

Join a writers' group or community to further enhance your writing journey. Participating in a local writers' group offers a supportive network where you can share your work, receive constructive criticism, and learn from fellow writers. Connecting with like-minded individuals who share your passion for writing can inspire and motivate you to push the boundaries of your creativity (Bleiweiss, 2023).

Understanding your publishing options is crucial as you navigate the writing industry. Educate yourself about the differences between self-publishing, hybrid, and traditional publishing. Each path has its advantages and considerations. Self-publishing grants you more control but requires self-management and attention to detail. Hybrid publishing balances self-publishing and traditional publishing, providing some professional support while allowing for creative freedom. Traditional publishing involves collaborating with a publisher who handles various aspects of the publishing process, from editing to distribution.

If you choose self-publishing, ensure a high-quality production by investing in professional editing and cover design. Remember, the presentation of your book can significantly impact its reception. Seek professional assistance or consider tapping into local resources such as college English and Art departments or senior programs like the Osher Lifelong Learning Institute (OLLI) (Bleiweiss, 2023).

Securing a literary agent can be immensely beneficial for those pursuing traditional publishing. Many publishers only accept manuscripts submitted by recognized literary agents. An agent can advocate for you throughout the publishing process, negotiate deals, and explore opportunities like foreign releases and film/TV adaptations. Research agents who specialize in your genre and craft personalized query letters when approaching them.

Crafting an outstanding query letter is essential to grab the attention of literary agents. Customize each letter to cater to their interests, highlighting why your book is unique. Provide a captivating synopsis, draw comparisons to similar books, and mention your social media presence to showcase your platform, identify your target readership, and include endorsements from other writers. For seniors, emphasize that this would be your first published book at your age, as it can generate publicity and interest.

In today's digital age, social media is vital in book marketing. Engage extensively with platforms like Instagram, Twitter, Facebook, and TikTok to build a following of potential readers. Target demographics that align with your book's genre and themes. Join writers' groups on these platforms for networking, support, and exchanging ideas (Bleiweiss, 2023).

As you embark on this journey to build a successful writing career, remember that persistence, passion, and continuous improvement are your allies. Embrace the challenges, embrace your unique voice, and let your words captivate the hearts and minds of readers worldwide. The world eagerly awaits the stories only you can tell.

Setting Realistic Goals

Writing a book is incredibly challenging, and the pressure to produce a great book adds even more difficulty. To ensure success in completing your book or other writing projects, it is crucial to establish tangible and achievable writing goals. These goals will serve as a blueprint, keeping you on track and motivated throughout the writing process. Next, we will explore seven tips for creating and sticking to your writing goals (Beasley, 2022).

Develop realistic goals.

Setting unrealistic goals will only lead to discouragement and hinder your progress. Rushing the writing process by setting unattainable goals can be counterproductive. Instead, focus on developing smaller, achievable goals you can consistently work toward. Consider your daily schedule, commitments, and responsibilities, and set realistic writing goals that align with your available time and energy.

- Helpful daily writing habits include:
- Write approximately 1,500 words every day.
- Allocate two to three dedicated hours at a specific time each day for writing.
- Aim to complete one chapter per week.
- Set aside time to read books by authors you admire, as this can inspire new ideas.
- Practice journaling or capturing detailed notes for future reference.
- Engage in meditation or reflection to encourage deep thinking.

Add specific metrics to your goals.

Vague goals need more clarity and make it easier to track progress (Beasley, 2022). Adding specific metrics to your goals will make them measurable and provide clear milestones. For example, rather than setting a goal to write more each day, specify a target of writing 1,000 words daily. Similarly, replace generic goals like "Become a better writer" with measurable objectives such as "Read one book per month" or "Complete two writing courses this year" (Beasley, 2022). Measurable goals enable you to monitor your progress and celebrate achievements.

Track your progress to stay motivated and gauge how far you've come.

Use calendars, project management software, or online tools like Asana to set goals and record achievements. Regularly review your progress to stay focused and adjust your approach if necessary. Consider scheduling periodic meetings with yourself to assess your progress at monthly or quarterly intervals.

Writing a book requires not just effort but also dedicated time.

To ensure you have enough time to write a high-quality book, prioritize your writing goals. Life's demands can easily overshadow your writing aspirations, so it's important to recognize that your writing dream is significant. Use a priority matrix to identify urgent tasks and allocate time specifically for writing. By prioritizing your writing, you honor your passion and increase your chances of achieving your goals.

Seek inspiration when the going gets tough.

While passion for writing may drive you, there will be times when motivation wanes, or external factors weigh you down. During such moments, seek inspiration and motivation from various sources. Read books similar to the one you're writing, explore literary journals for short stories or narrative essays, or access online scripts of your favorite movies if you're writing a screenplay. Additionally, join local writing groups or book clubs to connect with like-minded individuals. Engaging with fellow writers and learning from successful authors can reignite your motivation (Beasley, 2022).

Obtain feedback from trusted individuals.

Someone holding you accountable can significantly enhance your chances of achieving your writing goals. Share your goals with a friend, family member, or fellow writer who can provide support, encouragement, and occasional check-ins. Alternatively, join online writing groups where members share similar goals and can offer feedback on your work.

Do regular progress checks.

Regular progress updates with an accountability partner will keep you motivated and on track. Celebrate your milestones and accomplishments along the way to maintain enthusiasm and momentum.

Networking and Collaboration

You're partly correct if you've chosen a freelance writing career with the idea of working independently and undisturbed. However, if you want to make money as a writer, effective networking with other writers and editors is crucial.

Rather than viewing other writers as competition, consider writing a team sport, with editors as the most valuable players. Networking with like-minded writers creates a support system for sharing ideas, navigating low-paying content mills, and increasing visibility in a crowded market (Fitzgerald, 2017). Networking also opens doors to more work and income opportunities. Referring clients to trusted writers in your network when you're unavailable or when a project falls outside your expertise benefits both the client and the writer.

However, networking extends beyond writers and includes selling ideas, services, and products. Networking is vital to successful selling, as any salesperson will tell you. Writers must also market themselves, making it essential to build relationships with editors. Editors play a crucial role in the publication process, sifting through pitches and ensuring quality. To prove your capabilities and get published, it's vital to establish amicable relationships with the editors you pitch (Fitzgerald, 2017).

A mutually respectful relationship with editors leads to growth as they challenge and encourage you to improve your writing prowess. When pitching to editors, be professional, sincere, and efficient. Rejection is expected in the writing profession, so always thank editors for their time and consider requesting feedback, but don't expect it. Never speak ill of editors or take rejection personally. Rejection from one editor can lead to opportunities with another.

To expand your network, consider the following tactics:

- Assemble an all-star team. Expand your network to include professionals related

to your writing focus. For example, connect with web designers and developers if you're a website copywriter. This allows for mutual referrals and creates a seamless experience for clients.
- Join networks and get involved. Online communities, forums, social media groups, and local writer's groups provide opportunities to connect with peers in your niche.
- Participate in webinars or host your own. Attend webinars to engage with writers from around the world and share ideas. Consider hosting webinars or creating a community based on your expertise and experience.

As a freelance writer, it's crucial to be pleasant to work with, as there will always be another freelancer who is (Fitzgerald, 2017). Strive to advocate for other freelancers, and you'll discover a more extensive support network than you imagined.

Tips for Staying Motivated

- Writing a book can be exciting but challenging, especially when finding the motivation to get started and stay on track. In this section, I'll share valuable tips to help you stay motivated throughout your writing journey.

- Develop a daily habit of writing, even when you don't feel like it. Set achievable goals, such as writing a certain number of words or a page daily. Consistency builds momentum and makes the creative process more accessible. By the end of the year, you'll have a substantial body of work. For faster progress, consider writing a chapter each day. Make your writing time a daily habit by scheduling it at the same time each day.
- Avoid the temptation to edit while writing. Editing interrupts your creative flow and hampers progress. Instead, focus on getting your ideas down on paper and save the editing for later. Embrace the power of progress and keep writing until you finish the entire book (Tracy, 2022).
- Create a distraction-free environment for your writing. Minimize outside interruptions by turning off your phone, setting a "do not disturb" sign, or using a white noise machine to filter out

background noise. Devote your full attention to the writing process and strive to achieve a flow state.

- If you're feeling blocked or overwhelmed, don't be afraid to take breaks. Step away from your book for a few days, but set a date to resume writing. Giving yourself a deadline helps maintain accountability. Sometimes a change of environment or writing in a different setting can reignite your motivation.
- Draw inspiration from successful authors and their works. Think about how they support their ideas through analogies or real-life examples. Analyze the techniques they use, and consider applying them to your book. Additionally, explore the methods employed by celebrities who often work with ghostwriters to brainstorm ideas and gather examples.
- If you struggle to write, try speaking your thoughts aloud, like conversing with a friend. Write down the words that come naturally while expressing your ideas. Imagine explaining your book to a friend and conveying the message you want to

deliver. Talking through your book's problems casually can help overcome writer's block.

- Challenge yourself with creative writing prompts to stimulate your imagination. Describe your surroundings in detail, observe the world like an explorer, or use random words from a dictionary to inspire haikus or quotes from your characters. Explore various writing prompts to jumpstart your creativity and motivation. You can also find inspiration from motivational quotes (Tracy, 2022).

Key Takeaways

Finding unwavering motivation throughout the book-writing process can be a daunting task. There will inevitably be days when you don't feel like writing or the words refuse to flow effortlessly onto the page. However, by implementing diverse tools and techniques, you can persist and stay motivated even during those challenging times.

One of the most effective strategies is to develop a consistent writing routine. Set aside dedicated time each day or week specifically for writing. Treat it as a non-negotiable commitment, just like any other necessary appointment. Establishing a routine creates a sense of discipline and structure that helps overcome resistance and procrastination. Even if you don't feel inspired, sitting down and putting words on the page becomes a habit that gradually builds momentum.

It's crucial to separate the processes of writing and editing. Many writers get trapped in a cycle of self-criticism and perfectionism while trying to write their first draft. By allowing yourself to write without judgment, you can overcome the fear of producing imperfect work. Remember, the first draft is meant to be rough and imperfect. Editing comes later, during the revision stage. You can tap into your creativity and keep the writing process flowing by permitting yourself to write freely.

Eliminating distractions is another crucial element in maintaining motivation. Find a quiet space where you can focus without interruptions. Turn off notifications on your phone or computer and create a conducive environment for writing. Use productivity apps or website blockers to prevent distractions from social media or other online temptations. Creating a dedicated workspace and minimizing external interruptions will help you focus on your writing goals.

Taking regular breaks is important to avoid burnout and maintain motivation. Writing for long stretches without breaks can lead to mental fatigue and diminishing returns. Schedule short breaks during your writing sessions to recharge and rejuvenate. Use this time to stretch, take a walk, or engage in activities that inspire you. Sometimes stepping away from your writing for a brief period can lead to fresh insights and renewed motivation when you return.

Seeking inspiration from others can also reignite your motivation. Read books in your genre or explore different genres to discover new ideas and writing styles. Engage with the works of authors you admire, analyze their techniques, and let their words fuel your creativity. Join writing communities or attend literary events to connect with fellow writers and gain insights from their experiences. Sharing your struggles and successes with others who understand the writing journey can provide the support and inspiration you need to keep going.

Creative writing prompts can be a valuable tool to overcome writer's block and spark new ideas. Use prompts to explore different themes, characters, or settings. They can serve as a jumping-off point for your writing and help you overcome any resistance or mental blocks you may encounter. Writing exercises and prompts can also help you develop your writing skills and experiment with different styles.

Remember, the writing process can be challenging, and there will be times when staying motivated feels challenging. However, you can persevere and accomplish your writing goals by implementing these strategies—developing a writing routine, separating writing and editing, eliminating distractions, taking breaks, seeking inspiration from others, engaging in conversation with your book, and using creative writing prompts. So be not discouraged in the face of adversity or uncertainty.

Embrace these tools, dear writer, for they are your allies in this noble pursuit. Keep writing; each stroke of the pen brings you closer to the literary horizons you envision. Trust in the transformative power of your dedication and hard work, for they will guide you toward the summit of success, where your stories will shine like stars in the vast expanse of the literary universe.

FINAL THOUGHTS AND NEXT STEPS FOR FAST DRAFTING SUCCESS

Fast drafting is an efficient approach to writing that prioritizes speed and momentum over perfection. It involves quickly getting words on the page without self-editing or overthinking. Remember the following tips:

- Set a writing schedule. Establish a consistent writing routine and dedicate time to your fast drafting sessions. Whether it's early mornings, late nights, or specific blocks of time during the day, having a schedule helps you stay committed and focused.
- Embrace imperfection. Fast drafting is not about producing flawless prose from the

start. Give yourself permission to write messily, make mistakes, and leave gaps. Remember that the goal is to generate content rapidly, which can be refined in subsequent revisions.

- Silence your inner critic. During the fast drafting phase, silence your inner critic and ignore the urge to self-edit. Avoid going back to revise or perfect sentences as you write. Instead, keep pushing forward and let the words flow freely.
- Write in bursts. Aim for short bursts of focused writing instead of laboring over a single sentence or paragraph. Set a timer for 10–15 minutes and challenge yourself to write as much as possible within that time frame. This technique helps overcome writer's block and encourages a steady flow of ideas.
- Use prompts and outlines. Utilize writing prompts or outlines to provide structure and guidance during fast drafting. Prompts can spark ideas and keep momentum, while outlines offer a roadmap of key points or plot events to help you stay on track.

- Don't get derailed by research. While research is essential, it can slow down the fast drafting process. When encountering a research-related question, please make a note to revisit it during the revision phase and keep writing without getting sidetracked.
- Embrace creativity and intuition. Fast drafting allows your creativity and intuition to take the lead. Trust your instincts, let your imagination soar, and explore unexpected paths and ideas. This approach often leads to fresh and innovative storytelling.
- Celebrate progress. Recognize and celebrate your progress during fast drafting. Each word written brings you closer to your final goal. Acknowledge your accomplishments, no matter how small, to stay motivated and inspired.

By incorporating these techniques into your fast drafting process, you can overcome the barriers of self-doubt and perfectionism, allowing your creativity to flow freely and bringing your ideas to life on the page. Remember, the beauty of fast drafting lies in the freedom to write without constraints, enabling you to uncover the true essence of your story.

Encouragement to Keep Writing

No one wakes up daily feeling motivated to write, not even authors with bestsellers. There will be days when you don't feel like staring at a blank page. But as someone who has been through it, here's my advice: Push through and write anyway, even on those unmotivated days. Otherwise, you might fall into a cycle of procrastination. A day of not feeling like writing can quickly turn into two, then ten until you give up.

Many authors give up after their first, second, or even third attempt at writing a book, mainly because they lost their motivation and succumbed to procrastination or fear. If you want to publish a book, you must dig deep and find the motivation to write daily, even if it feels terrible or you hate it. The only way to become a better writer and finish your book is to push through those difficult moments.

- Don't confuse motivation with passion. Waiting to feel passionate about your writing will hinder your progress. Passion comes and goes, so don't rely on it. No matter how you feel, start writing.

- Outline first. Before diving into writing, outline your ideas to have a clear blueprint. An outline helps you gather relevant ideas and acts as a defense against fear and writer's block.
- Create small, attainable goals. Instead of setting high word count goals, you can easily achieve smaller ones. Consistency is key, so write between 500 and 2,000 words daily.
- Make it a daily practice. Establish a writing routine by picking a designated writing time and place. By making writing a daily habit, it becomes harder to procrastinate.
- Don't strive for perfection—get words on the page. Avoid getting stuck in pursuing perfection. Write a "vomit draft" without editing or overthinking. Embrace the imperfect first draft and focus on capturing your ideas.
- Focus on the reader. Keep your readers in mind and remember that your book aims to solve their problems or provide value. Please write in a way that is

simple, direct, and centered around their needs.

- Practice self-care. Take good care of your physiological, psychological, and emotional wellness. Prioritize sleep, exercise, healthy eating, and activities that rejuvenate you. Writing should be part of a balanced life, not an exhaustive endeavor.
- Announce your book. If external accountability motivates you, announce your intention to write a book to friends and family or on social media. Embrace the pressure and positive feedback that comes with sharing your goal.
- Recognize and face your fear. Acknowledge and confront your fears of inadequacy or judgment. Write them down, and overcome them by pushing through. Remember that your story is worth telling.

By applying these techniques, you can motivate yourself to write even when you don't feel like it and ultimately reach your goal of finishing your book.

Final Thoughts

Writing is not just a mere task; it is an extraordinary journey that allows you to become a master storyteller, an architect of emotions, and a conduit for your unique perspective to reach the world.

You can take readers to other worlds via your writing, elicit strong feelings, and leave a lasting impression on their hearts and minds. As you embark on this creative endeavor, you must recognize that developing good writing habits and disciplined approaches will significantly contribute to your success as an author. Just as a painter refines their brushstrokes or a musician perfects their melodies, honing your writing skills and techniques will enable you to create captivating narratives that resonate with your readers.

Embrace the power of imagery, for it allows you to paint vivid pictures in the minds of your audience. Harness the ability to describe sights, sounds, smells, tastes, and textures with such precision that your readers can practically feel immersed in the world you have created. Through carefully selected words and sensory details, you can create a multi-dimensional experience that captivates and engages your readers profoundly.

Belief in yourself and your abilities is paramount on this writing journey. Embrace the challenges that arise along the way, for they are not stumbling blocks but stepping stones toward growth and learning. Embrace the moments of self-doubt, for they allow you to push beyond your perceived limitations and discover the reservoirs of creativity within you. Trust that your unique voice and perspective have value and can make a difference in your readers' lives.

Commitment is the backbone of every successful writer. Stay dedicated to your craft, investing time and effort into sharpening your skills. Seek opportunities to learn and grow, whether through workshops, courses, or simply immersing yourself in the works of other talented authors. Explore different genres, experiment with various writing styles, and push the boundaries of your creativity. Remember that writing is a lifelong journey; there is always room for improvement and exploration.

Above all, write with passion and authenticity. Let your words flow from the depths of your being, infused with your unique experiences, emotions, and perspectives. Don't be afraid to be vulnerable and open, for it is through authenticity that you forge a genuine connection with your readers. Your voice, your truth, and your passion are the ingredients that breathe life into your writing and make it resonate with others.

As you navigate this remarkable journey's twists and turns, embrace the written word's beauty and power. Remember that you can touch hearts, inspire minds, and leave an indelible legacy through your writing with each stroke of your pen or keystroke on your keyboard. So, write fearlessly, write passionately, and let your voice soar on the wings of imagination. The world is waiting to be captivated by your words.

RESOURCES FOR WRITERS

Vellum is a premium book formatting software providing authors a simple way to create professional-looking eBooks.
Formats professional-grade eBooks and create print-ready files.
Pros: User-friendly, high-quality outputs, one-time purchase.
Cons: Only available for MacOS, more expensive than other options. Can subscribe to Mac in Cloud
mojosiedlak.com/vellum
mojosiedlak.com/macincloud

Atticus is a book formatting software developed by author Dave Chesson, simplifying the process of creating professional books.

Creates beautiful eBooks and print layouts.
Pros: Easy to use, multiple format options, one-time fee.
Cons: Newer software, the potential for bugs.
mojosiedlak.com/Atticus

Fiverr is a global online freelancer marketplace for authors needing affordable, diverse services.
Provides affordable cover design, editing, and marketing services.
Pros: Wide variety of services, transparent pricing.
Cons: Quality varies by provider.
mojosiedlak.com/fiverr

Reedsy is a marketplace for publishing professionals, connecting authors with quality editors, designers, and marketers.
Connects authors with vetted industry professionals.
Pros: Wide range of services, quality control.
Cons: High costs compared to non-vetted freelancers.
mojosiedlak.com/Reedsy

Writing is a passion and an instrument to express your voice and let the world know what's on your mind. Embrace the joy of creation, celebrate your achievements, and find fulfillment in storytelling.

Remember, my dear writers, that your words can touch hearts, inspire minds, and ignite the imagination. Embrace the resources available, seek feedback, and never stop honing your craft.

Embark upon the literary odyssey that is your writer's journey, for it is as extraordinary and singular as the tales you weave. Embrace the wondrous path ahead as you immerse yourself in the artistry of words, unwavering in your dedication and unyielding in your resolve.

May your prose dance upon the pages, imprinting upon the very fabric of our world, leaving an indelible legacy for all who dare to venture into the labyrinth of your creation.

BIBLIOGRAPHY

Aragon, M. (2021, September 22). How to edit a book: 8 step guide + mistakes to avoid. Self Publishing School. https://self-publishingschool.com/how-to-edit-a-book/

Beasley, M. (2022, December 20). 7 tips for setting achievable writing goals - 2023. Writer's Hive. https://writershivemedia.com/tips-for-setting-achievable-writing-goals/

Bleiweiss, R. (2023, February 22). 15 tips for starting your writing career later in life. https://www.writersdigest.com/be-inspired/15-tips-for-starting-your-writing-career-later-in-life

Bradshaw, C. (2020, September 25). 7 quick tips for mastering pacing in your story. Writer's Edit. https://writersedit.com/fiction-writing/7-quick-tips-for-mastering-pacing-in-your-story/

Ciara, C. (2018, April 27). How to create a productive writing environment. Ciara Conlon. https://ciaraconlon.com/2018/create-productive-writing-environment/

Corbett, D. (2011, April 12). How to craft compelling characters. Writer's Digest. https://www.writersdigest.com/improve-my-writing/hooked-on-a-feeling

11 powerful book promotion ideas for self-published authors. (2023). Editage. https://www.editage.com/book-editing-services-articles/11-Powerful-book-promotion-ideas-for-self-published-authors

Fitzgerald, E. (2017, September 11). How to network your way into a successful writing career. The Write Life. https://thewritelife.com/network-into-a-writing-career/

Gibbins-Klein, M. (2016, January 25). 10 things to consider

when choosing a publisher. Publishing Talk. https://www.publishingtalk.org/get-published/10-things-to-consider-when-choosing-a-publisher/

Hodges, P. (2017, January 17). 10 essential tips to improve your writing style. The Write Practice. https://thewritepractice.-com/writing-style/

How to outline a story: 7 steps to creating your book outline. (2022, December 19). Reedsy Blog. https://blog.reedsy.-com/how-to-outline-a-book/

How to write a great plot. (2023, March 23). Literacy Ideas. https://literacyideas.com/how-to-write-a-great-plot/

Jenkins, J. (2020, August 7). The Hero's Journey: How to use this classic story structure. Jerry Jenkins. https://jerryjenkins.-com/heros-journey/

Jenkins, J. (2022, January 18). How to create a character profile: A step-by-step guide for beginners. Jerry Jenkins. https://jerryjenkins.com/character-profile/

Jordan. (2021, October 20). How to create tension in a story: 8 simple steps. Now Novel. https://www.nownovel.-com/blog/create-tension-writing/

Kieffer, K. (2016, September 9). Should you fast-draft your novel? well-storied. https://www.well-storied.com/blog/fast-drafting

MasterClass. (2021a, August 19). 13 freewriting prompts to help break your writer's block. MasterClass. https://www.mas-terclass.com/articles/freewriting-prompts-to-help-break-your-writers-block

MasterClass. (2021b, August 23). How to create a consistent writing schedule: 10 tips for writers. MasterClass. (2021, Au-gust 23a). https://www.masterclass.com/articles/how-to-cre-ate-a-consistent-writing-schedule

MasterClass. (2021c, August 23). How to use the five senses in your writing. MasterClass. https://www.masterclass.-com/articles/how-to-use-the-five-senses-in-your-writing

MasterClass. (2021d, August 30). How to develop your writing ideas. MasterClass. https://www.masterclass.com/articles/how-to-develop-your-writing-ideas

MasterClass. (2021e, September 10). 7 common plot devices and how to use them in your writing. MasterClass. https://www.masterclass.com/articles/common-plot-devices-and-how-to-use-them-in-your-writing

Matesic, A. (2022, October 9). Common writing mistakes to spot when self editing. Alyssa Matesic. https://www.alyssamatesic.com/free-writing-resources/self-editing-tips-for-common-mistakes

Max, T. (2021, November 4). 9 ways to boost your writing motivation (That actually work). Scribe Media. https://scribemedia.com/writing-motivation/

Mohr, J. (2021, January 8). The importance of consistency: How to keep the details straight when writing your novel. TCK Publishing. https://www.tckpublishing.com/the-importance-of-consistency-in-writing/

Morgan, K. (2016, September 29). Strategies for how to overcome the challenges of writing a paper. Seattle pi. https://education.seattlepi.com/strategies-overcome-challenges-writing-paper-5463.html

Mustful, C. (n.d.). The publishing process: A step-by-step overview. History Through Fiction. https://www.historythroughfiction.com/blog/the-publishing-process

Patterson, A. (2018, May 4). 10 cliffhangers that make readers turn the page. Writers Write. https://www.writerswrite.co.za/10-cliffhangers-that-make-readers-turn-the-page/

Pope, B. (2022, May 30). How to write dialogue: Formatting, examples, & tips. Self-Publishing School. https://self-publishingschool.com/how-to-write-dialogue/

Reedsy Team. (2022, April 21). How to write faster: 8 strategies for Productivity. Reedsy. https://blog.reedsy.com/how-to-write-faster/

Ren. (2019, April 1). Fast-drafting & hitting word count goals. Ren Hutchings. https://www.renhutchings.com/post/tips-for-fast-drafting-hitting-word-count-goals

Revising your paper. (2021, July 21). Writer's Center: Eastern Washington University. https://research.ewu.edu/writers_-center_revising_paper

Robson, H. (2014, October). The big benefits for writing fast. American Writers & Artists Institute. https://www.awai.-com/2014/10/the-big-benefits-for-writing-fast/

Setting the scene in story writing. (n.d.). BBC. https://www.b-bc.co.uk/bitesize/topics/zx339j6/articles/z6w2wnb

Tips for creating an effective book marketing plan. (2019, September 20). Smith Publicity. https://www.smithpublicity.-com/2019/09/creating-an-effective-book-marketing-plan/

Tracy, B. (2022, November 11). 7 tips to stay motivated when writing a book. Brian Tracy International. https://www.bri-antracy.com/blog/writing/how-to-stay-motivated-when-writing-a-book/

The 22 best writing tools of 2023: A guide for writers. (2023, February 7). Reedsy Blog. https://blog.reedsy.com/writing-tools/

Utgaard, A. (2017, June 9). 20 incredibly useful resources for aspiring authors. Medium. https://writingcooperative.com/16-incredibly-useful-resources-for-aspiring-authors-730012a4d91c

Valentine, M. (2019, January 30). Pacing in storytelling - 12 common problems and fixes. Book Editing Associates. https://www.book-editing.com/pacing-fiction-storytelling/

Weiland, K. M. (2016). Creating character arcs: The masterful author's guide to uniting story structure, plot, and character development. Penforasword

When to ask for feedback of novel? Stack Exchange. (2018, June 3). https://writing.stackexchange.com/questions/21687/when-to-ask-for-feedback-of-novel

Writer's Relief. (2022, April 15). How to build tension and suspense in your writing. Medium. https://writersrelief.medium.com/how-to-build-tension-and-suspense-in-your-writing-d8c5ba6bf392

mojosiedlak.com/youtubechannel

ABOUT THE AUTHOR

Monique Joiner Siedlak: Author, Witch, Warrior.

With storytelling infused with mysticism, modern paganism, and new age spirituality, Monique awakens your potential. Initiated into the craft at 20, her 80+ books explore the magick and mysteries of life.

A Long Island native, she now calls Southeast Poland home but remains a citizen of Mother Earth.

Beyond her pen, Monique craves new experiences and cherishes nature, advocating for animal welfare.

Join her captivating journey as she transports you to enchanting realms and empowers your own transformative path. Unleash the dormant magic within and embrace the extraordinary with Monique Joiner Siedlak's evocative words.

To find out more about Monique artistically, spiritually, and personally, feel free to visit her **official website.**

www.mojosiedlak.com

facebook.com/mojosiedlak
twitter.com/mojosiedlak
instagram.com/mojosiedlak
youtube.com/@MoniqueJoinerSiedlak_Author
tiktok.com/@mojosiedlak
bookbub.com/authors/monique-joiner-siedlak
pinterest.com/mojosiedlak

African Spirituality Beliefs and Practices

Hoodoo
Seven African Powers: The Orishas
Cooking for the Orishas
Lucumi: The Ways of Santeria
Voodoo of Louisiana
Haitian Vodou
Orishas of Trinidad
Connecting with your Ancestors
Blood Magick
The Orishas
Vodun: West Africa's Spiritual Life
Marie Laveau: Life of a Voodoo Queen
Candomblé: Dancing for the God
Umbanda
Exploring the Rich and Diverse World

The Elemental Magic Series

Wiccan Basics
Candle Magick
Wiccan Spells
Love Spells
Abundance Spells
Herb Magick
Moon Magick

Creating Your Own Spells
Gypsy Magic
Protection Magick
Celtic Magick
Shamanic Magick
Crystal Magic

Divination Magic for Beginners
Divination with Runes
Divination with Diloggún
Divination with Osteomancy
Divination with the Tarot
Divination with Stones

The Spiritual Empowerment Series
Creative Visualization
Astral Projection for Beginners
Meditation for Beginners
Reiki for Beginners
Manifesting With the Law of Attraction
Time Bound
Healing Animals with Reiki
Being an Empath Today
Crystal Healing
Communicating with Your Spirit Guides

Life on Fire

Healing Your Inner Child

Change Your Life

Raising Your Vibe

Get a Handle on Life

Get a Handle on Stress

Get a Handle on Anxiety

Get a Handle on Depression

Get a Handle on Procrastination

The Holistic Yoga and Wellness Series

Yoga for Beginners

Yoga for Stress

Yoga for Back Pain

Yoga for Weight Loss

Yoga for Flexibility

Yoga for Advanced Beginners

Yoga for Fitness

Yoga for Runners

Yoga for Energy

Yoga for Your Sex Life

Yoga to Beat Depression and Anxiety

Yoga for Menstruation

Yoga to Detox Your Body

Yoga to Tone Your Body

The DIY Body Care Series

Creating Your Own Body Butter
Creating Your Own Body Scrub
Creating Your Own Body Spray

SUPPORT ME BY LEAVING A REVIEW!

goodreads

BookBub

Made in the USA
Middletown, DE
09 September 2025